10. 9. 8.

7. 6. 5.

4. 3. 2.

1. 0

Jennifer S. LeBlanc, MS

Launching for Revenue

How to Launch Your Product,
Service or Company
for Maximum Growth

Launching for Revenue

How to Launch Your Product, Service or Company
for Maximum Growth

Published by

HAL HOUSE

Copyright © 2018

by Jennifer S. LeBlanc

Editor: Kay Paumier
Cover design, book design and creative direction: Gabriela Martínez

ISBN: 978-1-7321639-0-4

DESIGNED AND PRINTED IN THE UNITED STATES OF AMERICA

*Dedicated to Barbara and Robert for always believing in me,
and to David and Rachel for supporting me
as I spent countless evenings and weekends writing.*

"There is nothing more difficult to take in hand, more perilous to conduct, or more uncertain in its success, than to take the lead in the introduction of a new order of things."

Niccolò Machiavelli,
political philosopher
and historian

Acknowledgements

It takes a village to raise a company – and to write a book. After many years of formulating the ideas in this book, I have so many people to thank and acknowledge.

First my family. Thanks to my husband David Hedley, for believing in me and the vision for this book. Thanks especially for that day on the water when I realized that I had to write this book before I could get the next one out ... the one I'd already half written. That was a hard decision, but it's been worth it.

Thanks to my daughter, Rachel Anderson, for inspiring me to be all that I can be. You are a light in this world and the world is better because of you.

And thanks to my mother, Barbara LeBlanc, for being my inspiration for what is possible and for endlessly picking me up when I fell, and when I still do. I can never thank you enough.

Several coaches had a role in creating and shaping the ideas in this book. Thanks to Kate Purmal for encouraging me to write down the way that I instinctively know what companies need to succeed in their launches. Thanks also to Lisa Goldman, Kim Fulcher, Susan Kim, Belanie Dishong and Don Ramer, for encouraging me to use my full voice. And to Karen Hagewood and Kathryn Bowsher for always being in my corner.

Ideas do not come out of nowhere and these concepts were built of experience with some fantastic bosses and mentors. I refer especially to Katy Fairman, Beth Miller-Thiel, Jay Fulcher, Jeff Reid, Lon Fiala, Lydia Barrett, Chris Byrne, Libby Frisby, Linda Adreveno and Carlos Schuler. Thank you for all that you taught me.

And thanks to the clients who helped shape and refine these concepts, especially Karen Ambrogi, Ozlem Coday, Brittany Conrad, Mary Cortani, Dana Dornsife, Tim Enger, Stacy English, Ege Ertem, Sharon Lustig, Mukund Mohan, Michelle O'Connor, Prashant Sharma, Jennifer Ruddock, and Jodi Sievers.

I'd like to acknowledge my sister authors who shared their experiences with writing and publishing their books. Anne Janzer, Linda Popky and Lisa Stambaugh, bless you.

Of course this book required input and patience by the key members of my ThinkResults team. Thanks to Gabriela Martínez and the graphics team, who designed the book cover and the layout. To Kay Paumier, who provided valuable structural feedback and editing to make sure the concepts were clear. And to Sean Hodrick, who helped with the research for the social media chapter. I'd also like to acknowledge the rest of the team—Jennifer Berkley Jackson, Deb Siegle, Olivia Dippon, Julie Gouldsberry and Michelle Panulla—who kept things on track as I focused more and more on writing. And thanks to Dave Nielsen, Lisa Stambaugh, Harry Miller and Kevin Heney who helped me formulate the early concepts that led to the 10 Elements.

I'd also like to acknowledge some people who are no longer with us, including my grandmother, Iris Pring, for giving me the writing bug, and my father and grandfather, Robert LeBlanc and Ronald Pring, for always believing I could do it.

Last but not least, I want to give a shout out to Mrs. Norwood, my 10th grade English teacher, who cried when I said I would study science at college. I wish I could show her I have come full circle and am writing again.

Onward,

Jenn LeBlanc

Praise for *Launching for Revenue*

"Launching for Revenue is a clear and simple guide to the perplexing and chaotic period that is launch time. Do not go into those new and uncharted waters without this guide by your side."

– Anne Janzer, author of *Subscription Marketing*

"The 10 Elements of Launch contained in this book gives marketers a step-by-step guide for how to bring something new to market — the right way. The concepts are clear, concise and immediately applicable."

– Jay Fulcher, chairman and CEO, Zenefits

"When it comes time to launch, whether it's a new product, a new company, or even something new inside a large company as an intrapreneur, this is the book to read!"

– Linda Popky, author of *Marketing Above the Noise* and president of Leverage2 Market Associates

"This book outlines a clear and concise method for determining your most valuable brand identity and your easiest go to market strategy in order to generate revenue quickly."

– Jennifer Ruddock, SVP, Investor Relations and Corporate Affairs, Nektar Therapeutics

Table of Contents

Introduction to the 10 Critical Launch Elements

If you are launching a new product, service or company, chances are good that you won't succeed.

Research shows that up to 35–80% of all launches fail. That's a big range because "success" is notoriously hard to measure, leading to controversy about the exact percentage. Even 35%, however, is an unacceptable failure rate, especially given the significant resources required for each product, service or company launch.

While these statistics apply specifically to product launches — the most well-studied form of launch — one can easily hypothesize that these percentages would apply equally to service and company launches. In fact, half of all new U.S. companies fail within their first five years. Within the startup community, the failure rate is even worse, at least for high-growth tech startups, with a 92% failure rate within the first three years. These are not heartening statistics.

Launches fail for a variety of reasons and at a variety of times, sometimes shortly after launch, sometimes within the first year and sometimes even before the launch happens.

On the other hand, the market clearly is full of new products, services and companies that are changing our lives in big and small ways. Some launches are successful despite the overwhelmingly negative odds.

So what makes the difference between failure and success? That is a question I have been obsessed with for more than two decades now.

After leading and participating in dozens upon dozens of launches, commissioning proprietary research about the launch process, and being a keen observer of both successful and failed launches, I realized that the reasons for the high failure rate can be identified, isolated and studied. Once I realized this, I made it my focus to get this information to as many people as possible, hence this book.

As a result of this study and analysis, we have developed the ThinkResults Launch Readiness Assessment method, which identifies the top 10 most critical elements of a successful launch. This method reveals how ready a company is to launch, and also identifies the biggest areas of risk. As a result, companies can predict and course correct their launch plan to maximize their chances of a successful launch.

Defining the 10 Launch Elements

The 10 launch elements were carefully chosen based on our analysis of failed and successful launches. We have seen launches fail as a result of poor execution of one or more of the following 10 critical elements:

1. The Offering (Product/Service/Company)
2. Positioning
3. Name
4. Logo

5. Website

6. Sales Strategy

7. Content Strategy

8. Social Strategy

9. Team

10. Funding

Of course, all these elements don't need to be perfect, but the majority need to be in good form to execute a successful launch. We usually define a successful launch as one that meets the revenue targets, either in terms of sales or an acquisition.

You may define success differently and that's fine. Just be sure that you do take the time to define success before you start. Are you looking to primarily increase awareness about your product, service or company? Or are you looking for hard measurements of success, such as an increase in leads or in new customers or in revenue? Be sure to define exactly what your measures of success are before you start. More on this in the final chapter about putting together your Launch Action Plan.

We will go into each element of launch success in detail so you will have a clear idea of how ready your initiative is in terms of launch. Case studies, key questions, and self-assessment checklists will help you develop a clear idea of which elements need the most attention to ensure a successful launch.

Research Findings: Key Learnings from Peers

Several years ago, I wanted to better understand whether the trends we were seeing with our clients were unique to them or reflected trends in the broader economy.

So we designed a survey with our research partner, The Insight Advantage, to get some quantitative answers from B2B leaders across a variety of industries, including high tech/software (25%), consumer goods (13%), and healthcare/medical (13%). Nearly half of the respondents had revenues of greater than $500,000. Regarding their roles, 37% were in management and 31% were in marketing.

Several findings were consistent with what we typically see during launch projects. First, in terms of results achieved, 50% reported that the company name was better known. Awareness is the first step in the purchase process so this is a critical result. Additionally, 46% reported that they had acquired new customers, and 21% reported that existing customers had increased purchases of existing products/services and also of new products/services. These are all consistent and common strategic objectives for launching a new offering, so it was great to see these results reported by our respondents.

The other set of statistics that we think is important from this research and also consistent with our clients' experiences, was regarding timelines. We asked people how long their last few launches were and 64% responded that they were typically one to three months.

We then asked them how long they would have liked the launch timeline to be to increase the success, and 50% said the ideal prep time was three to six months. I cannot stress this finding enough.

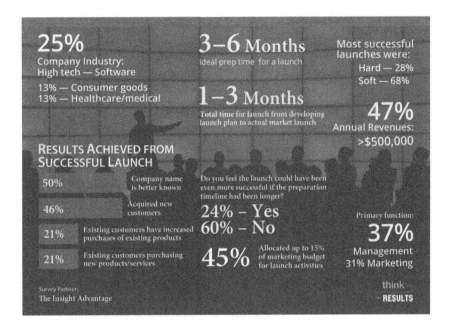

While it's possible to do a launch in a few weeks or months (and we have done successful launches in as little as two weeks), I do not recommend this as a typical or in any way ideal timeline. Depending on how ready you are to launch and how much foundational work you need, generally, a launch takes three to six months.

We live and work in Silicon Valley where that is considered an eternity, yet it truly takes that long to maximize your chances of a successful launch — and to maximize your revenue from the launch.

Regardless of how much time you have before launch day, the information in this book can help you make sure you get the most value — and revenue — from your launch project.

Who Should Read this Book?

This book is intended for founders, marketers and would-be marketers who are responsible for launching, or who want to launch a company, product or service.

You may be the CEO or CMO of a startup, or a Director or VP of Marketing in a larger company. Whether you are an entrepreneur or an intrapreneur in a large company trying to start something new, the common thread is that you are a change agent. You are either launching a new company with an associated product or service, or you are working from the inside out in a big company to bring something new to the market.

Some of you may be responsible for re-launching a company, product or service. There are some specific reasons for, and challenges associated with, relaunching and this book will help you address those smoothly.

This book may also be helpful for those of you who are not in marketing (engineers, I'm talking to you). This book will provide insight into the launch or relaunch process, and the factors that your marketing team is grappling with as they move through this process. This may be useful in how and what you decide to offer as technical marketing support to the team during launch.

How to Use this Book

This book is meant to be a practical guide to launch, with quizzes at the end of each chapter, so please jump around as you see fit. If you are short on time, our free online quiz takes less than two minutes (Link: https://thinkresultsmarketing.com/launch-readiness-assessment-quiz/).

Taking this quiz before reading through the book may give you an early glimpse into which elements will be the most important to your launch. Then you can use those specific chapters in the book to determine your launch strategy, and fill out the worksheet in the last chapter, Launch Action Plan. This would be how to hack this book, for those of you short on time.

For those of you that prefer to get a deeper understanding of the process, want relevant examples to spur your thinking, or want to learn how to set up more success for future launches, read through each chapter. Questions at the end of each chapter will help you quantitatively assess each of your 10 launch elements.

By the end of the book, you will have 10 element scores, each out of a possible score of 10, so the scores neatly add up to 100. Then use the worksheet in the final chapter, the Launch Action Plan chapter, to formulate your specific launch strategy, based on your unique launch needs.

Off we go!

1.

Developing the Offering

Let's start with the first step: developing the offering. This may the company itself, which usually means you are also launching either a new product or service. Or you may be launching a new product or service within an existing company or product line.

Let's start with the product offering and how to develop that for launch. I'll handle the specifics of launching a service later in this chapter.

This is the part that all the engineers love … the product discussion. There's a popular saying here in Silicon Valley: "Build a disruptive product and the product will sell itself." That, my friends, is the thinking of many a ruined entrepreneur.

Products do not sell themselves. To be successful, they need to solve a problem or enhance life, be designed for a specific market, be tested in that market and refined accordingly.

The first thing to consider before launching your new product is "Is it FULLY functional?" Before you can answer "yes" to this question, you must be able to answer the following questions positively:

1. **Is the product fully developed and does it work in the environments most users prefer?**

   For example, if it's an online service, does it work on all the major browsers (not just your engineering team's favorite)? Your engineering team may hate working with Microsoft® Internet Explorer and, while it's true that the overall internet usage of IE is just over 4%, it is a commonly mandated corporate browser. If you are targeting a corporate audience, you may find your overall audience usage is much higher so IE can't be ignored as a result of the engineering team's personal preferences. This is but one example of the kind of customer-centric thinking that will need to go into the product development.

2. **Can people learn how to use the product without taking a week-long course?**

   Long, long gone are the days of functionality over form in engineering. Design matters now thankfully make the difference between wildly successful products and ones that never get past five users (three if you exclude your mom and your brother).

3. **Have you received user feedback from a cross-section of your target market? And have you integrated that feedback into your design?**

   Designing for just you and/or your engineering team is a great place to start. Great companies can be founded on solving problems the founders had in their own lives. But do not fool yourself into believing that what is obvious to you and your engineers is obvious to your target market. Your prospective customers have busy, complicated lives, and your product or service is a solution to but one of the challenges in their lives. Seek out honest feedback from your target market and listen carefully.

Note: When getting user feedback, do not lead the witness. One of my favorite hacks is to hand your product to a variety of user personas* in your target market and ask them to make it work. Video record their responses. Resist the temptation to show them how this button or that function works. Simply watch. See where they stumble in taking the next step or completing a process. This has long been a staple tool for Intuit, for example, and has helped them develop several successful products.

User personas are profiles of the types of people who buy your product. For example, one of your buyer persona profiles may the Chief Technology Officer in a high-tech company. It's important that you understand what the pains are for each of the personas who will buy, or influence, the buying decision. We will get into more detail on personas in Chapter 2, the Positioning element of this book.

4. **Does the product work consistently?**

Do not launch if it only works on Tuesday or when your engineers have a specific setup for demos working. That product is not ready. It must be stable. A product only gets one chance to make a first impression — don't blow it with a buggy product.

If you can answer yes to these four questions, then you can honestly say that your product is fully developed from a marketing and customer perspective — at least developed enough to launch. Of course, there will be iterations, refinements and even whole new generations of products along the way as you launch and learn more from your market. Never stop getting feedback into your organization.

But What About a Minimally Viable Product?

Much has been written about developing an MVP (minimally viable product) and there is a lot of controversy on this topic. The term "minimally viable product" was coined by Frank Robinson and made popular by Steve Blank and Eric Ries in *Lean Startup*. Ideally, it refers to developing the minimal product you need to sell the vision, without over-engineering it.

I have seen many companies try to use this as a cover for launching a buggy, unstable and hard-to-use product (see the four questions above). The point that is often missed in these cases is that emphasis should not be on the "minimally" part. It should be on the VIABLE part. Go back to the four questions to determine if your product passes that test. If not, it is not even yet an MVP. It's a prototype.

For a product to be minimally viable, you have to be able to convince someone to buy it. It must be saleable.

There is little value in over-engineering a product as well, which is why the MVP concept is so popular when it is not abused as a cover for sloppy product design. Years ago, I was sitting with the engineering team of a large software company talking about the long list of features they were working on for an upcoming product release. I shared with them some of the customer feedback on the three to four key features customers kept asking for when using our current product.

The engineering team's response was: "But those are easy to do. We'd rather work on these cool features." None of those cool features were on the top-requested list. If we had focused on the "easy" features, we could have released the product much earlier and given customers a better experience over the existing product.

Strike the balance between a minimally VIABLE product and an over-engineered one with features that users will rarely use.

Put Your Users' Needs First

At the risk of sounding like a broken record, you must design products for actual users. Be specific when defining your ideal customers. For example, are they:

- Toddlers between 2–4

- Older homebound people who need help managing simple tasks

- Women juggling full-time jobs and children

- Introverted engineers

- First-time home buyers trying to navigate the sales process

- Urban folks trying to get from Point A to Point B safely and quickly

- Travelers looking for a local experience

- The list goes on ...

Know your target market. Create personas and study individuals who fit that persona, especially as they struggle to solve the problem you are trying to solve with your service or product. Why? Because if you design products in a vacuum, launching them will be a long and expensive process.

Case Study:
The Importance of User Knowledge and User Interface Design

Let's look at an example to illustrate the points above. A small tech toy company came to us several years ago with a complete product. It was an app that you played with via your phone and a 3-D printed version of a device that came with it to really unlock the fun.

The product had great IP (intellectual property) protection and the product was stable. Its problem? The brilliant and curious design team had essentially created a science project. They wanted to see what the accelerometers in an iPhone could do when released from the constraints of how fast you can move your hand.

As I said, the product worked beautifully. It did, however, require at least 20 minutes of verbal instruction to be able to use the free app. That was the first major problem.

The second problem was the founders weren't sure who their target market was. Was it toddlers with loose hand dexterity? Teens who would want to share the experience with their friends? Or mature technophiles like themselves who were super curious?

After limited user testing with a sampling of people representing those groups, it became clear that the target market should be older children and teens who would be able to explore the full creative potential of this app and device, and who would most likely want to share it.

With that information in hand, we made some minor tweaks to the app. Before this all of the buttons, even those rarely used, were the same color and size. Consistently in every video of user testing where we handed the phone and the device to people, they would stop dead when they opened the app because they didn't know where or how to start.

So we changed the user interface in a way that highlighted the first few buttons teenagers would press to get started. We also added some simple in-app help details, a mini in-app Get Started Guide to show people what buttons unlocked which functions, and highlighted how to share your new creation, which is important for this demographic. This interface change took a few hours of coding time and made a huge difference for new users.

Then, with a new user friendly interface in hand and knowledge of the target market, we took the product off to the Chicago Toy and Game Show. The technology was quickly licensed to a major global toy company to integrate into new products.

Clearly defining the product market and making sure that market could easily use the product and see its value unlocked its potential.

Ensuring the Product Is Protected Legally

I am not a lawyer, yet I understand having the appropriate product protections and working with the appropriate agencies are critical to launching well. If your product makes a health claim, you must, for example, work with the FDA to ensure compliance with U.S. laws about health products. If you have certain chemicals or even particular elements in your product, you must also be in compliance with the EPA regulations.

One of our clients was a medical textiles company and we were making health claims about protecting patients from healthcare-acquired infections (such as those from surgery, intubation tubes and other in-hospital procedures). The product contained an element that reduced bacterial growth. That element was regulated by the EPA. As a result, we were in close conversations with both agencies to ensure that the launch of the product would not be hampered by regulatory issues.

In terms of IP protection, make sure you are working with an experienced IP lawyer. This is a tricky area of law and there are many ways to put a fence around what you have created, not all of which are effective. There's nothing worse than launching a product and discovering that you are entangled in a messy legal situation because you are infringing on an existing product.

Special Guidelines for Launching Services

Some additional guidance for those of you launching services. Although much of the testing and user experience discussed won't apply directly to you, a lot of the thinking is still relevant. Even with services, you need to clearly define your target market and ideal persona, and then have processes in place to make sure you are listening and removing any stickiness in your sales and service delivery process. And the IP guidelines also apply to services.

One area that needs additional attention in service launches is ensuring you can smoothly deliver those services once they are launched. You may need to hire more people to support the new services or reorganize the team you currently have. These changes should be put into place well before the launch.

By making sure your product (or service) is fully functional, designed for specific users to solve specific problems, and protected by the appropriate IP fences, you will be in a good position to successfully launch. Of course, there are other elements to consider, but if your product doesn't work, or you can't effectively deliver your service, nothing else will work in your launch.

Offering Rating Instructions

Please answer the following questions, giving up to two points for each of the five questions below.

Here's a guide on how to rate your answer:

0	1	2
We are seriously lacking	We're ok here, could be better	Got this one nailed

Is the product/service/offering:

a. Fully functional?	/2
b. Easy for your target market to use?	/2
c. Covered by appropriate legal protections and/or complies with regulatory guidelines?	/2
d. Covered by appropriate IP filings?	/2
e. Qualitative rating	/2

Total: ____ out of 10

Use the qualitative rating to increase or decrease your score to get what seems "right" on a scale of one to ten. This is a chance to soften your ratings if your score for this element seems too low.

This will give you a rating for this element. Transfer this score to the Launch Elements table on page 158.

Once you have scored all 10 elements in this book, add up the individual scores to get your Launch Readiness Score. These questions are also repeated in the final chapter for your convenience, so you have them all in one place there.

2.

Defining the Positioning

In response to the ever-increasing pressure to deliver ROI immediately, marketers (and founders) often skip over the important strategic step of defining their target customer and clearly articulating the brand's position, value proposition, and key messages to attract those key persona profiles. There just doesn't seem to be time to invest in this, especially in startup or launch mode.

Even more worrisome, the company may take the time to complete the persona and the messaging and positioning work, but fail to discuss it and gain agreement from the management team and key stakeholders. Then they wonder why they can't get the new website or brochure approved in a reasonable time.

Developing a strategic, clearly defined and articulated one-page brand story, which contains your brand positioning statement, differentiated value proposition, and key messages, is the most important first step in any new branding, rebranding, or repositioning project. The next step is to gain agreement from management and key stakeholders so that the resulting statements will actually be used consistently across the organization.

Going through this process saves time, money and a lot of frustration during the implementation phase because the overall brand position and key messages have already been vetted. I have found that doing this strategy work up front makes it so much easier to develop all the other communications, whether it's a website, landing page, ad or lead-generation campaign.

Persona Profiles: Why Defining Your Target Audience Is Your First Step

Before you even start developing your positioning, you need to clearly articulate who your product or service is for ideally. You may not be completely familiar with persona profiles, but they are essentially a tool to create a clear description of your ideal buyer and, if the sale is complex (as it often is in B2B environments), the main influencers. You may have more than one main buyer and even multiple influencers per buyer. Start with your largest segment and build from there.

Having great persona profiles allows your marketing team to build marketing that truly engages and inspires your target customer. It's like taking an entire segment and boiling it down to one person. So much easier to talk to one person than an audience of 10,000, right?

A persona is a composite profile that summarizes the needs and wants of your ideal buyer. We like to give them real names and photos so we can connect with the persona on an emotional level. Here is an example of a CIO persona we developed for a client.

CIO: Sam (40–55 years)

S am has a successful progressive career in global enterprise companies. She has influence, a good reputation, and is looking to further make her mark.

Profile	Her pain?	What are her triggers to take action?
• Woman or man • 100% responsible for the company's technology • Has an MBA • May be non-technical or "old-technical" • Feels "behind the 8-ball" in developing a digital strategy • Decision-maker but builds multi-level buy-in and consensus • Wants to be seen as a thought leader	• Worried about what she doesn't know/what she's missing; failure • Wrong info in the wrong hands • Company at risk of being seen as "dated," not relevant or current • Losing key team members to competition, downsizing and changing technical skillset requirements • Needs to create her department as a profit center • Navigating the solution to reducing costs and meeting expectations from CEO/Board	• Aligning with the CEO/Board • Wants to know she's on the right path to digital transformation • Doesn't want to be late to market • Learns she can partner with and leverage trustworthy partner • Reads article/case study • Attends a conference and learns how another company significantly shortened development time and time-to-market • Hears from a CIO colleague about their experience at an executive event • Team recommendations

You'll notice several things about this persona profile. First the picture. We always include a picture to make the profile come alive. I want to be talking to that person directly.

Secondly, we summarize the profile. The executive summary of the persona, essentially.

Then we have the detailed profile section, where we get into psychographic details about our target buyer, helping us to target the right imagery and language for this person.

The next section lists the typical pains and obstacles this person experiences in his or her role. The final column lists the typical triggers that prompt this person to take action. Combined, these two columns enable us as marketers to design campaigns that address their pains and move the target buyer towards a decision.

Clearly, you could develop multiple persona profiles. Start with the most important and add more as you need them. Review and update the profiles every 6 to 12 months, depending on how fast your industry is changing. New triggers and new pains can crop up, especially in the technology industry.

Defining Successful Positioning and Messaging

So what exactly is positioning and messaging and how can we do it well? First we need define our terms as some people use these terms differently, depending on the industry.

The four elements of the Brand DNA Blueprint

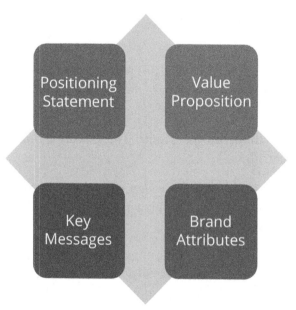

As the diagram suggests, we consider the positioning statement, the value proposition, the key messages and the brand attributes as part of what we call the Brand DNA. Let's look at each element:

1. Positioning Statement

Your positioning statement defines the space in the market that you want to own in the future. This is not where you are now, but rather where you want to be. This is your organizational North Star.

As well as being a critical marketing statement, the positioning statement is also an important strategic reference. When done well, it can help you determine whether to invest in a certain product line, do a certain acquisition or pursue some other company-defining initiative.

Some organizations use the positioning statement as an external statement while many do not. It is a matter of preference.

2. Value Proposition

Closely associated with positioning is your value proposition, sometimes referred to as your "elevator pitch." This is the core of your message framework and where you want to spend most of your creative energy.

Your value proposition is a one- to two-sentence summary of the compelling reason why your customer wants to buy your product or service solution. Make it simple, bold and emotional.

This is an external message and one that will be repeated everywhere as it explains the value of your company and tells its story in just a few words. This is the heart of the message framework, so spend the most time on this section of the message framework when developing it.

3. Key Messages

The key messages amplify and provide more detail on your value proposition. Ideally you should have no more three short messages – or even just three words.

These messages should be backed up with facts and figures that prove the point. People buy with emotion and justify with facts. Use the value proposition to sell with emotion and the key message proof points to give them those much-needed facts to justify the decision they have already made. This way, you are using neuroscience in your favor.

4. Brand Attributes

The brand attributes are essentially the brand's personality characteristics. What makes your company unique? How does it express its personality in the world?

Brand attributes are not typically shared externally. More often they are used to define the tone and voice in the content you develop for sales situations, social media channels, and other content marketing initiatives.

These brand attributes can be extremely helpful in guiding the choice of images over time to ensure that the visual message echoes your intended brand personality. Your creative director and/or art director will be grateful for these, trust me.

Shown is a blank template of the framework we use during the Brand DNA Method process to develop a company's positioning.

Positioning Statement The market position you want to own in the future. (15–20 words)	
Value Proposition Compelling reason for customers to buy your product/service. What are your key differentiators? (1–2 sentences)	

Key Messages	• Key Message 1
	  - Proof point
	
	• Key Message 2
	  - Proof point
	
	• Key Message 3
	  - Proof point

Brand Personality Attributes:	

Your brand positioning statement, value proposition, key messages and brand attributes need to fit on one page as in the template above. Why? Because this forces you to be succinct, which is valuable in itself.

This document then becomes your one-page brand story that is articulated in every communication with your target audience (e.g., website, advertisements, blogs, social media, sales presentations, news releases, collateral, and other communication vehicles). This is how you can achieve the marketing nirvana of consistency across all media. This is especially critical when you are a small company. Being consistent across all channels will make you seem larger than you are and will magnify your impact.

Using this strategic framework, it is a simple matter of developing the standard variations of company descriptions (or messaging) most commonly requested: the one-liner, the one paragraph or "boilerplate" often used at the end of press releases, and the longer half-page or so full company description.

What Strategic Positioning Is Not

Now a word or two about what this strategic positioning document is not. It is not the whole story. Your website, social media channels and sales presentations give you plenty of room to articulate the details of your story. But these longer communications should rely on the brand story document for the foundation of the communication. They simply build on it.

Also, this brand story document is not a panacea for all corporate brands simultaneously. If your company has several product or service lines, there should be one overall corporate brand story, and a brand story document for each major product or service. Each individual product/service brand story should echo the overall corporate brand story, and explain the specifics of the product or service.

And your positioning document is not messaging. That is derived from this foundational Brand DNA document, as I mentioned earlier.

Four Steps to Great Positioning and Messaging

A positioning and messaging exercise can be done poorly or it can be done superbly. Like most other good things in life, you get out of it what you put into it.

To develop great positioning and then messaging, there are four hallmarks toward which you should aim. When first starting out as a company, it is difficult to hit all four of these on the head. Great brands, however, hit all four of these hallmarks well.

Keep it Simple	Be Bold

Get Emotional	Deliver Credibility
Kaiser Permanente "Thrive" campaign	❝ We are a proven partner, with an average of one drug approval and five successful Investigational New Drug Applications every year. ❞

1. Keep It Simple

This old adage is so true ... keep it simple. We're all busy and, with so many talented marketers vying ever more smartly for our attention, we just can't absorb complex information.

A research report from the University of California, San Diego, indicated that the average American consumes 34 gigabytes of content and 100,000 words of information a day. That's enough to overwhelm a typical laptop in a week. The report was in 2009, so I can imagine it's much higher now even.

Keep your positioning simple and short. There will be time later for more detailed information about your company, product or service.

BMW, for example, has kept it simple for more than 30 years. They've been "The Ultimate Driving Machine" for all these years, and that is one reason why that tagline, which defines their brand, is so memorable. It hasn't changed, so we don't need to relearn a new fact about BMWs. When we want a sleek car that feels the road, we know which dealership to visit. Simple.

We've often joked on our team that you know your messaging is tight when you can get it all into a Google ad. Seriously. With two 30-character headlines, and an 80-character description line, crafting a great on-message Google ad is a Zen-like exercise in branding elegance. This is often where we find out how "tight" the messaging is — or isn't.

This is particularly challenging for our clients who must live under the scrutiny of the FDA or the EPA. But always a great mental exercise nonetheless.

2. Be Bold

Use unusual words, phrases, or images when describing your brand. It helps you to stand out from the crowd. A rebranding or repositioning campaign is a big investment. Don't waste it on being the same as everyone else. As Seth Godin advises in his book, be a Purple Cow.

Seth Godin is a great author and always a fun read. I will summarize the thesis of his book *Purple Cow: Transform Your Business by Being Remarkable* with this analogy he uses in it: If you are driving along the highway and see a herd of cattle, you just keep going, probably not even looking at the cattle. But if that herd of cattle contained something bold, something unusual, like a purple cow, you and everyone else would be pulling over and snapping pictures of this unusual cow, giving it a lot more of your attention. Be a purple cow. Be memorable.

Be bold in your brand promise. Stick your neck out — if this makes you nervous, stop and examine why. Because if you can't keep a promise made to customers, you have a bigger problem on your hands than needing to re-brand or reposition your company. The best positioning is driven by the over-arching corporate strategy, and therefore a brand promise should be easy to make and keep. After all, your whole company is built around it, right?

We worked with a small user-experience design firm in San Francisco years ago to help them craft a more compelling value proposition.

After working through the Brand DNA method, we came up with "We design and deliver the perfect product user experience." This is a clear, simple and bold promise to their clients — and they deliver on it every day.

3. Get Emotional

When developing your brand story, remember that we are all human, no matter what industry we're in or how many degrees your target audience has. It's a fact of human nature that we all love a good story. Tell one.

Appeal to something larger than the brand, a higher state of being. Re-set the rules of the game against your competition by appealing to some attribute we'd all like to think we possess, such as being a great parent, being a good friend, or being stronger, faster, or better than we actually are.

Kaiser Permanente, a national health maintenance organization (HMO), embarked on a brilliant positioning campaign years ago, based on the human desire to not just survive our day-to-day lives, but to thrive. The radio ads emphasize all the things Kaiser Permanente stood for, like green beans and spinach, exercise, sunscreen, deep breathing, and antioxidants. Print ads emphasize the word "thrive" and feature people lounging in hammocks and generally enjoying life.

Now, HMOs typically are not seen as proactive, and are seen as being more concerned with cost-cutting than with health. Kaiser Permanente sought to change that by emphasizing something beyond their actual brand — this higher state of health where we can all thrive. Now that's a bold and emotional brand promise that has had lasting appeal.

4. Be Credible

Your new market position and value proposition should be credible and achievable relative to your current position. When defining your key messages, use facts and figures to heighten your credibility.

For example, a client wanted to position his company brand as a trusted leader in biopharma services, especially for venture-backed firms. He backed up his new position and value proposition with key messages like "We are a proven partner, with an average of one drug approval and five successful Investigational New Drug (IND) applications every year."

Using this credibility fact, he hooked his potential clients with his positioning statement and value proposition and then sold them with compelling facts and figures. Getting a drug approved, or even getting the IND into the FDA is a monumental task. Having a partner that has done that successfully and at that pace is phenomenal.

A Few Words About the Term "Differentiated"

Many books have been written on the subject of positioning. The Al Ries and Jack Trout's classic, *Positioning: The Battle for Your Mind*, is a great place to start. Much of the current thinking is that the positioning needs to be "differentiated."

Maybe that's clear in other parts of the U.S., but here in Silicon Valley, that term seems to be sublimated into the term "disruptive." (Don't get me started on the overuse of that term.) It's more common that HOW a company does what it does is what differentiates them, not WHAT it does. You do not need to create a disruptive product or service in order to be differentiated. You just need to do it in a way that separates you from the rest of the pack.

Take Nordstrom's for example. On the surface, what they do is generic. They are a department store. How they deliver that experience is what differentiates them. We will see how long their brand of superior customer service lasts in the age of dying brick-and-mortar retail, but I predict they will last much longer than department stores where you can't find a single person to answer questions, let alone help you buy products. You do not need to disrupt an entire industry to be successful.

That said, when working with clients on their positioning, I am always on the lookout for how we can create a new playing field for them versus carving out a corner of an existing and often crowded playing field.

7UP® did this famously in the late '60s with their "Un-Cola" positioning. Although it connects them with "cola" of which Coca-Cola® and Pepsi® are the dominant brands, it separated the field of sodas into "colas" and "other than colas." This both took advantage of the overwhelming market share and mind dominance that colas have in the soda market and brilliantly created a new playing field which 7UP used to dramatically increase its sales.

Try to create positioning that is not copycat or only slightly better than the competition. Create positioning that either distances you from the pack or gives you a whole new playing field that you can defend. Coke could not, for an example, become an "Un-Cola," so 7UP effectively "depositioned" both Coke and Pepsi.

A Few Words for Readers from Large Companies

Those of you working as intrapreneurs inside large companies will need to do some specific things when launching or repositioning your product that are unique to larger companies.

Several years ago, I listened to a Harvard Business School panel here in Silicon Valley that included Chris Yeh, SVP, Product and Platform at Box and Jay Chitnis, Sr. Director Solutions Marketing at EMC, representing both the upstart and the established leader in enterprise cloud storage.

Both panelists stressed the need to reposition themselves from the "race-to-the-bottom" cloud storage vendor to document workflow and collaboration solutions. Moving the conversation from the individual user to the C-level in terms of the overall efficiency of the organization was considered essential to ensure these companies remained viable in a competitive environment. Given that both companies had healthy and growing revenues, I found their focus on repositioning fascinating.

Effecting a successful repositioning in a larger organization requires special skill and care. You will need to gather input from the various people who will be affected by the change. Why? Because I guarantee you that other people will see things you would never see on your own.

We all live in our little bubbles of information and input. And the higher you are in a company, the smaller that flow of information becomes about what is really happening in your company. You may know a lot more than the average worker about customers and partners, but even that may not be true.

As a result of your position of power, people carefully filter what they tell you. You need to actively seek out input, relying on people you know you can trust and perhaps even pushing the fact-finding down to lower-level generals so you can get real feedback.

One way to gather this critical feedback on your repositioning is to socialize the idea. Toss the idea out during hallway conversations, before or after meetings with key people you trust. Find a way to informally get feedback, responses and additional ideas about the change you want to make. During this socializing process, hopefully someone will tell you if you are about to jump off a cliff you can't see because of your position.

The second reason it is important to gather feedback is that, if people feel included in the development of the change you are seeking, they will be much more likely to support that change. As a bonus, you may also get some interesting feedback that helps to refine and strengthen your idea.

Either way, socializing the idea of the change before implementing it makes the whole process smoother. In a large company, any kind of significant change, including a repositioning, should be done after a healthy period of socialization.

Make the Investment in Great Positioning and Messaging

In summary, defining or repositioning a brand is a long-term investment, so make the time to effectively complete a thoughtful strategic positioning document and then the associated standard messaging. This will ultimately save you significant time and money.

The keys to success in positioning and messaging are to keep it simple, be bold, get emotional and be credible. Then make sure that your key stakeholders buy into it, and be consistent in developing your marketing materials. You'll soon be well on your way to a successful and profitable brand launch.

Value Proposition Exercise from Guy Kawasaki

Here's one of my favorite exercises on crafting a clear value proposition, taken from Guy Kawasaki's *Art of the Start 2.0*.

Step 1: Write a one-paragraph description of your customer's experience when she is using your product.

Step 2: Call up a customer and have her write a one-paragraph description of using your product.

Step 3: Compare the two descriptions. (I would add: distill the descriptions down to one or two sentences.)

Simple. Brilliant. Cuts to the heart of the matter.

Positioning Rating Instructions

Please answer the following questions, giving up to two points for each of the first three questions and up to four for the final, qualitative question.

Here's a guide on how to rate your answer:

0	1	2
We are seriously lacking	We're ok here, could be better	Got this one nailed

Do you have:

a. Clearly defined positioning?		/2
b. With a differentiated message?		/2
c. A message that resonates with your target audience?		/2
d. Qualitative rating		/4

Total: __ out of 10

Here is a guide for the qualitative evaluation:

0	1	2	3	4
We are seriously lacking	It's not terrible	We're ok here, could be better	We are getting there, still missing something	Got this one nailed

Use the qualitative rating to increase or decrease your score to get what seems "right" on a scale of one to ten. This is a chance to soften your ratings if your score for this element seems too low.

This will give you a rating for this element. Transfer this score to the Launch Elements table on page 158.

Once you have scored all 10 elements in this book, add up the individual scores to get your Launch Readiness Score. These questions are also repeated in the final chapter for your convenience, so you have them all in one place there.

3.

Choosing a Name (or a New Name)

So you've decided to have a … company (or a product or service). One of the first (of many) decisions is what to name it.

This is an important, and often emotional, decision that is no less crucial than naming a baby. Except that when naming a baby, there can be more than one Brittany or Jennifer names given out each year (trust me on the multiple Jennifer thing). Not so for companies and brand names. These must be unique in your category, which makes the whole process more challenging.

This naming business can be especially daunting as there are many horror stories of naming or renaming initiatives gone wrong.

Case Study:
Incubus Runners Go Too Fast

One of my favorite examples comes from Reebok, a company with copious resources. In the late 1990s, Reebok developed a specialized running shoe for women called the Incubus. Simple enough name, easy to pronounce (at least in English) and easy to remember. So far, so good.

The product successfully made it to store shelves when it was quickly recalled and Reebok issued profuse apologies. Turns out, Incubus is a male demon that violates women in their sleep. Not exactly the kind of image you want when selling a product to women!

Lesson learned? At the very least, research the meaning of the new name. At best, be sure to do linguistic and cultural testing of the name in your major target markets.

Getting the Name (or New Name) Right

Since so much rides on getting the name right, what do you need to know when undertaking a naming project? Here are our "Seven Golden Rules of Naming" to keep you out of hot water (most of the time). When evaluating your new name, consider whether the proposed name is:

1. ## Short — no more than two to three syllables

   If it's more than that, people will automatically shorten it and you'll be forced to adapt. Beverages and More has gradually adapted to being called by its once nickname, BevMo. That works fine but it would have been easier if they had made the name shorter to begin with. And no, one to three syllables does not mean four; it means one to three syllables. Period. (There are some specific linguistic situations in which you can have four syllables, but that is a nuanced decision for which I cannot give broad guidelines.)

2. **Memorable — some names are just so forgettable**

Typically names tend to be either very weird, like Zilinx, or very generic, like American Paint Supply. Make it something people will remember, something with style. For this reason, I have never understood why car manufacturers name their cars using numbers. Very arcane and hard to remember. Your company is distinct – make sure the name is too.

3. **Easy to pronounce**

If people can't figure out how to pronounce the name, that will make it harder to remember. Something that follows the natural rules of the English language works well.

4. **Not vulgar/negative in another language**

In this flat world, it's crucial that you have a good linguist look at your list of names. It's surprising sometimes what the translation can mean. A colleague of mine was involved in a near-miss example when she discovered (in time to change it thankfully) that the brand name chosen for the company's latest product referred to private male anatomy in slang French.

5. **Available with a good URL (domain name)**

This is so critical as you need the URL to match your company name. And, yes, all the good ones are taken. It's much easier to buy a new URL than it is to try to wrestle it away from someone who's squatting on your favorite new name. Check before you leap.

6. **Available in your category**

You will need to register your name within a certain category (hence you'll need legal help) and you need to be sure the name isn't already taken by someone else in the same category. If you've followed Rule #2, you should be fine. I haven't looked, but I'd be willing to bet that "American Paint Supply" already exists and that means that it's "taken" in the "paint supply" category. Check that in advance and don't wait until you're submitting for your new-business-entity documentation.

7. A word, not an acronym

This is a pet peeve of mine and one I see all the time. Folks say, "Well, what about IBM?" Yes, well, when you have billions of dollars to spend on marketing and branding, and several decades in which to establish that brand, go ahead and use an acronym. (By the way, IBM was created because everyone got tired of saying "International Business Machines" (10 syllables ... refer back to Rule #1).

Another big decision in the naming process is deciding whether you want a real word (or a close approximation) like Apple or Google, or are willing to flex to an imaginary word made from a combination of syllables, like Escalade. It is infinitely more difficult to find a real word or a variation of one that fills all the criteria above. So if you have your heart set on a real word or variation, you may have to give up on one of the rules above.

If you can confidently answer "yes" to all seven questions above, you probably have a good name. I'm assuming here that you have already engaged a lawyer to run the trademark question so you are clear on your freedom to operate under that name and any potential competitive issues.

Of course, there is much more to choosing a name than just these simple questions, but this is a great first-pass filter for your name candidates. Taking the time to evaluate your new name with these questions in mind will keep you on solid naming ground.

Case Study:
Protecting Your Name Can Be Costly

We received a call from a company that needed to do renaming project because they had run into trademark and competitive issues with their original name. A subsidiary had filed trademark rights to the name globally and was demanding $1.5M from the parent company to allow the parent brand to continue to use the name.

Even though it was the parent company's brand name, they had failed to file any basic legal protections to it. Consequently, they were left with some uncomfortable and expensive decisions.

Lesson learned? File at least the basic legal protections for your company name.

Case Study:
Back-of-Napkin and Startup Naming Issues

Another client had to rename because another company in their space challenged the client's "back-of-a-napkin name," which they had come up with over a beer. (Believe me, this happens more than you can possibly imagine.)

Although our client had been using the name for many years, the other company that had sent a cease-and-desist letter proved that they had been using the name before our client. The other company had been unaware of my client until we got involved as their marketing agency. We were in the midst of a successful awareness campaign and so their name was suddenly all over the national news (CBS, AOL, Huffington Post, Reuters, Time Magazine, ABC News and many others), drawing the attention of the other company.

As a result, we had to halt our campaign and the launch, and quickly rename and rebrand the company. Then we were able to continue with the original launch campaign to raise awareness about the company and its valuable life-saving technology.

This type of unfortunate situation is all too common in young enterprises. The name is generally chosen quickly and it sticks because it has cachet and appeals to the founders, who are more focused on product development than the finer details of naming or trademark rights. The name is often not put through even a basic naming screening process, let alone a thorough and rigorous vetting process, leading to an eventual renaming.

Lesson learned? At least do some simple online searches and check with the U.S. Patent and Trademark Office to be sure you have clearance to use your name in your category.

What About Renaming?

In addition to the more obvious concerns regarding naming a new brand, the rules that apply to choosing a good original name also apply to renaming a company or product. The three most common reasons for renaming are:

1. The company or brand has outgrown its original name

2. The company wants to move into new markets and a new name can help reposition it in the eyes of customers and clients

3. The company needs to put a negative brand association or scandal behind them

Number three isn't exactly a happy reason, but it is often a good reason to rename your company.

Another thing people often ask when facing a name-change decision is about their brand equity. My response is that brand equity is, and should be, much more than your name. And if you do the renaming correctly, your customers will transition to your new name much faster than you can imagine.

Generally, we find that, when the name change is handled correctly, customers cannot remember the original name within six to nine months of the change. Let's do a little experiment here. What was the former name of the consulting firm, Accenture? Or of the internet provider, Comcast? Or the former name of the car maker, Nissan?

People and their memories are much more plastic than we expect.

Renaming as a Repositioning Strategy

The two most common reasons for renaming are generally the most likely reasons why a company chooses to rename itself. Renaming your company is a strong signal to the outside world that reflects either that there have been massive internal changes or that there is change in direction or market, or both.

For example, I was responsible for executing on the name change of a biotech in the San Francisco Bay Area from its original name, Inhale (a great name for sure), to Nektar Therapeutics.

Inhale was founded on an inhaled insulin drug concept. At the time of the renaming, that product was still very viable and the company had several other inhaled products in development. However, Inhale had acquired two companies, neither of which were inhalable technologies. One company focused on powder technologies for oral drugs, and the other on a promising technology mostly for injectable drugs. Clearly Inhale as a name no longer represented everything the company did. Customers and partners prompted Inhale to change its name in an industry that typically doesn't take marketing very seriously at all. And so the name was changed and it marked the change in strategy that supports the company to this day.

Case Study:
Renaming Overstock.com to O.co and back to Overstock.com

In June 2011, Overstock.com renamed itself as O.co. The company returned to Overstock.com just three months after the branding change, after pushback from customers who didn't understand the name change.

At this point, the company had already spent millions of dollars on a six-year naming rights deal alone with the Oakland-Alameda County Coliseum, according to www.ragan.com. That doesn't include the likely millions spent on the rebranding project itself. That is one expensive naming mistake. As someone who lives close to this coliseum, naming that coliseum is a local joke. It's had more names in the last 20 years than a con artist.

Lesson learned? Make sure you thoroughly understand why you are renaming and communicate that thoroughly to key stakeholders, especially your customers. Or you may risk your whole investment and still not achieve the repositioning you were aiming for with the name change.

Renaming as a Result of a Scandal

In terms of the more painful reasons for renaming, a scandal, or even just a bad reputation, is sometimes a reason for a renaming. There are many examples through the years of this strategy including Philip Morris renaming itself to Altria, following a high-profile case against Philip Morris after a woman died from smoking and her family sued, and ValuJet's renaming to AirTran, following the crash of Flight 592 in 1996 where 110 passengers died.

Accenture is one example of a prescient name change. Andersen Consulting became Accenture early in 2001, just before a nasty scandal involving Arthur Andersen, the parent company, and Exxon's accounting problems in later 2001. That was a just-in-the-nick-of-time renaming that successfully removed Accenture from any of the negative brand halo effects of the demise of its parent company.

These kinds of naming projects can be extremely effective for the brand equity reasons I mentioned earlier. Although renaming is a painful pill to swallow, people care a whole lot less about your brand than you do. But this is actually good news because when you've transitioned properly to a new name, the scandal or negative brand equity remains in the past with the old name. As I mentioned earlier, it seems to take people just six to nine months to completely forget the old name.

In the last several years, I'm sure many great companies named after the beautiful and powerful goddess, Isis, have undertaken a renaming project, through no fault of their own or scandal. Renaming is a powerful tool.

Now that I've made the naming/renaming process sound daunting (unfortunately, it can be), remember, this is also a fun process and will be an important part of your corporate identity for many years to come. Also remember that the name does not make the company; the company makes the name. Over time, the name you choose will come to be infused with all the brand characteristics that represent your new company.

Naming Rating Instructions

Please answer the following questions, giving up to two points for each of the five questions below.

Here's a guide on how to rate your answer:

0	1	2
We are seriously lacking	We're ok here, could be better	Got this one nailed

Does your offering (product/service/company) have a name that:

a. Is memorable? Easy to say and spell?		/2
a. Has positive connotations?		/2
a. Has been tested in the major languages/markets in which you plan to sell?		/2
a. Is available in your category (trademark protection) and as a good URL?		/2
a. Qualitative rating		/2

Total: __ out of 10

Use the qualitative rating to increase or decrease your score to get what seems "right" on a scale of one to ten. This is a chance to soften your ratings if your score for this element seems too low.

This will give you a rating for this element. Transfer this score to the Launch Elements table on page 158.

Once you have scored all 10 elements in this book, add up the individual scores to get your Launch Readiness Score. These questions are also repeated in the final chapter for your convenience, so you have them all in one place there.

4.

Designing the Logo

The logo is an integral part of the brand. It is the public face of the brand every minute of every day. The logo needs to work hard every minute to stand out in the crowd, to withstand the test of time, and to support your overall communication objectives and the message you want in the marketplace.

Logo design needs to drive results. One of the biggest challenges of creating a logo is that it needs to distill all the facets of the company or brand down into a small design. Turning the full company story into a "simple" logo is simply hard work. We laugh about this because, at the end of a logo-development process, the logo design always seems simple and easy, and the choice so obvious. Yet the process rarely is. A great deal of research and thinking needs to go into a good logo design.

Here are some of the things we think about when designing a new logo or redesigning an existing one.

Is the Logo Visually Clean and Simple?

Generally, logos should contain up to three visual elements. Fewer is better. This is why making a "simple" logo is so hard. Distilling a company down to just a few elements is difficult intellectual work (and one of the reasons we so enjoy the challenge of logo design).

A key decision when designing a logo is whether it will be a wordmark logo where the name itself is the logo with no additional embellishment other than the font modifications. Or will you include a "bug," a visual enhancement, as part of the design. Here is an example of a wordmark logo:

ORACLE®

These logos are typically designed by either creating a custom font, or modifying an existing font such that the logo is no longer representative of that font. Wordmark logos tend to be clean and simple in their design.

Many logos opt to include a "bug" to embellish the name and add additional visual information. For comparison, in the same industry (ERP software) as Oracle, Workday opted for the addition of a bug to the name, the sunrise arc in a warm yellow orange to depict "the dawn of a new day in enterprise applications," according to Jeff Shadid, head of Workday Public Relations. Jeff also indicated that the combination of the yellow orange for the arc and a warm blue for the name were designed to balance the leadership, stability and tranquility of the blue with the positive energy and warmth of the orange, and to distance the Workday logo effectively from the competition.

Logo designs that included a "bug" as well as the logotype can also be simple and clean. The Workday logo example above has just two elements: the Workday name and the sunrise "bug."

Is the Logo Useable at All Sizes?

This point is frequently overlooked in the development or redesign of a logo and something we use as an important test of new designs at ThinkResults. Many logos can be blown up to work well on a billboard or tradeshow sign. Few, however, are tested to their smaller limits before a final logo is chosen. This is a big mistake. Most logo design processes show the logo about the size you would see on a business card, or as the only item on a PowerPoint slide.

This is NOT, however, how logos exist in the wild. They are used on business cards, in the lower corner of a PowerPoint slide, on a pen, on a cap, shrunk into 50 x 50 pixels on the LinkedIn logo preview, shown as a favicon (the little logo icon in the browser bar) at 16 x 16 pixels, and so on. You get the picture.

Here's a secret weapon to make sure the logo designs will really work when the logo is released to the wild. Shrink it down to its smallest size, the favicon (16 x 16 pixels) to see if it's still legible. (This is about the diameter of a head of a pencil eraser.) Also test the logo on all the typical social media formats, which are constantly changing. Many great designs fail miserably at this test. So toss those out at this point. If the logo design can't exist in the wild, it needs to be culled.

One of the hacks for the favicon, which is pretty darn small, is that sometimes you can just use the bug or other logo element be the favicon and not put the whole logo into that 16 x 16 pixel space.

Another thing to think about in terms of usability is the form factor. Years ago, logos were commonly rectangular because they were typically used on printed paper and then on webpages.

Today, it's better to design a logo to be more square, or at least a "squat rectangle." This is because most social media sites require the logo to fit into a square space. Again, if the logo contains a bug, this can sometimes be used on its own in social media. However, whenever possible, I prefer to see the whole logo used. If it's square or at least "square-ish," this will be possible.

Does the Logo Reflect the Brand Promise Well?

This is the final and most elusive of the logo criteria. The key to being able to answer this question is having solid criteria for the (re)design as well as a clear understanding of the brand promise before beginning the work.

Make sure that you have captured the specific criteria for the logo and have documented the brand promise for the logo before any design work begins. The general criteria discussed here in this chapter are important for every logo. Additionally, we discuss the objectives for the new or redesigned logo to determine if there are some additional criteria specific to that logo development. It's fairly common that people are expecting the new logo to meet some specific criteria. Make sure you know what those are first.

Once you have these logo development criteria in place and the initial logo concepts are developed, you can then assess how well each concept meets your criteria. In the process, you may toss out some criteria in the final decision because other criteria were so beautifully met. (See the enACT case study below as an example.) Having these criteria in place reduces the "but I like this one better" conversations and brings a more measureable and scientific framework for decision-making to an artistic process.

A few notes about the logo and brand promise. I've seen clients get all wrapped around a pole because the logo is "too simple" to convey the "full brand promise." They are right. But it is too much to expect a few visual elements to convey your full brand promise.

The logo is the crown jewel of your visual brand identity. However, other stones also exist in that crown, as does the structure of the crown itself. The logo plays a starring role, but it is not the only role, so don't expect your logo to tell the "full brand story." You will never get to a logo decision if that is one of your criteria.

Also remember that your logo, at the beginning, is an empty vessel. Perhaps the most famous of all logos, the Nike® swoosh, did NOT emerge with all that brand equity and meaning on day one. Over time, with lots of reinforcement of the brand promise through the delivery of great performance shoes to consumers, and millions spent on advertising, celebrity endorsements, retail outlet design, shoe design and other marketing, that swoosh is no longer an empty vessel.

Over time, your new logo will absorb and expand meaning from the customer experiences that you deliver through your brand. I'm a student of Zen philosophies. Your logo is everything (central to your brand identity) and nothing (an empty vessel in the beginning of its life). Let go, choose the logo that best meets the criteria above. Then go forth and make sure that you infuse it with fabulous brand experiences for your clients and customers.

Case Studies:
FedEx and Starbucks

There are tons of examples of poorly executed logos. I find it more useful to analyze successful, well-executed logos and especially redesigns. A logo redesign is a chance to give a brand a new life.

A classic example of a good logo is the FedEx logo. This is a typical wordmark logo without a bug, in purple and orange, which are complementary colors on the color wheel. Orange gives the purple energy and a sense of urgency. The one thing a lot of people don't always notice about this logo is the forward arrow, again emphasizing the speed and motion of the FedEx service, in the negative space between the "E" and the "x". Look closely between the "E" and the "x" and you will see the white arrow.

This logo would pass all the tests described above. I want to contrast this with another iconic logo that I would not have approved: the Starbucks logo.

For one thing, there are way more than three elements in this logo (her body, her face itself — with multiple elements — two arms, her two tails, numerous scales, six strands of hair, two stars, the logotype name, a white ring, a green ring, the inner white ring). Did I miss something? This logo would have failed the "clean and simple" test. This failure also means it fails the test of being useable at all sizes as it doesn't shrink down well. The monotone color does help somewhat.

Clearly, Starbucks has been massively successful despite the challenges of this logo. In the beginning, it did reflect the artsy coffeehouse vibe that it pioneered in the U.S., which is a good thing. And now, having spent billions in advertising, the limitations of this logo have been overcome.

Many of our clients do not have Starbucks-sized budgets and so need to make the right decisions from the beginning to ease their traction in the marketplace. Most marketing mistakes can be overcome with enough budget. However, it's generally best to do your work upfront and come up with a logo that doesn't need a gargantuan budget to succeed.

Case Study:
enACT Logo Redesign

Getting back to good logo design examples, I'll use a logo redesign we completed as part of an overall launch project for an energy management software company, enACT. The original logo was interesting visually, but had some problems in terms of long-term execution. This design, for example, would be difficult to reproduce any smaller than a business card, which is one of our logo design tests mentioned above.

This original logo contained the "e" and the "a" in enACT as part of its design in a deep, cool blue for the "e" and a vibrant orange for the "a" followed by the enACT name in black. In the original criteria for the redesign, developing a new logo that retained the "e" and the "a" in the design was designated as an important redesign criteria.

Original logo:

The CEO also wanted to move into the end-consumer space and wanted the logo to help carry the weight of that expansion and be more engaging and interesting. Another objective was to NOT use green too heavily as it is overused in the energy space.

So we set to work.

New logo:

This new logo contains the colors of the sky and the sun on a bright sunny day, evocative of happiness and the kinds of environmental protection that the company's software can deliver for end-consumers. The "en" is a warm sunny yellow and the "act" a bright sky blue. The colors are bright, engaging and attention-getting.

The "bug" is driving the momentum forwards and up, also signaling positive progress. It is slightly evocative of a butterfly without being sappy. It repeats the yellow and blue in the name in the wings of the design element, with a small touch of kelly green in the center where the blue and yellow wings overlap. This gives a nod to the energy focus of the company.

Unfortunately, the "e" and the "a" element was not preserved in this design. We had other designs that did but this was such a clear design winner, the CEO released that criteria during the design process. This logo has, however, been successful in helping enACT gain traction in the global consumer marketplace. enACT has also been recognized as one of the top 100 most interesting energy companies in the nation by the U.S. Department of Energy.

Overall, it was a successful logo redesign and this logo is out in the world driving results for enACT every day, carrying its new brand message out to consumers.

Case Study:
Operation Freedom Paws Logo Redesign

In 2012, we did a pro bono brand relaunch for Operation Freedom Paws (OFP). This work included a redesign of their initial logo.

To give some context, OFP is a local Bay Area nonprofit that gives mostly rescued shelter dogs new lives by matching them as service dogs with our returning veterans who have post-traumatic stress disorder (PTSD) and others with visible and invisible disabilities. The two train for nearly a year to become certified service dog teams and move back into a new normal in their lives. The operation is headed up by Mary Cortani, a 2012 CNN Hero, former Army dog trainer, and all-around amazing woman.

One of the first projects in the rebranding was to redesign and simplify their logo. The original design was beautiful yet complex. It told the entire brand story in one place. By now, you will know that's asking a lot of the logo and usually leads to unnecessary complexity.

We took the most essential elements, the dog profile (focused and at attention), the iconic red cross for help, and a simple blue circle to contain the elements, with the name around the outside in a larger font, just once. This simplification focuses the eye on the emotional connection and loyalty of a canine buddy.

The other elements in the logo (the 15 stars representing Mary's 15 years of military service, the six stripes representing her rank as staff sergeant) came out in the original website redesign work, freeing up the logo.

Another design element came out more in the copy and description of the services OFP offers. That element is the dog's tail which, in the original design, "breaks" the circle, representing the cycle of vigilance common in PTSD. We felt that, although this was important, it was a lot to explain visually. And containing the logo in a complete circle also tells the story of the wraparound services OFP offers its clients and tells it in a way that is easier to understand visually.

Before the redesign   After the redesign

The revised logo is much easier for the organization to use on T-shirts, caps, etched wine glasses and all the typical places a nonprofit logo often appears. And Mary, the executive director, absolutely loves it and now looks back at the old logo as "way too busy," even though she had been highly resistant to changing the original logo. That, by the way, is a common reaction to a logo change. During the redesign process, careful attention must be paid to the emotional attachment people (especially founders) often have to the original logos.

When to Redesign?

A few words about when to consider a redesign. Much like renaming, there are some clear times when a logo redesign makes sense:

1. **If you are renaming, you MUST do a logo redesign.**

    Trust me on this one. If you try to save money by skipping the logo redesign with the old name, your intent will be clear to everyone and will not reflect well on your company.

2. **If you want to reposition your company, and retain the current company name.**

    This is one of the clear times that a logo redesign makes perfect sense. A logo change is a great way to signal changes to the outside world.

3. **If your logo has become dated over time.**

    Morton Salt is a perfect example of this. The company has been in business for more than 100 years, and the logo and the Morton Salt Girl have evolved visually over time to remain fresh and relevant.

When doing a redesign, all the same rules apply as they do when doing a new design. Additionally, there will be more story, more heritage and more information to convey since the company is not new. Often a redesign is done to separate an existing company more from the competition. So the pressure is just that much more intense for a redesign than for a new logo.

Clearly there are many facets to developing a logo that will help it stand out from the crowd for your launch, and also stand the test of time. Using the above examples, think about your new/redesigned logo project and answer the following questions. Will your logo stand out? Will it last over time? Does it clearly (and simply) articulate your brand promise?

Most importantly, try not to make your logo carry too much of the brand's weight. That is the most common mistake I see in developing logos. The logo is important but it isn't everything.

Logo Rating Instructions

Please answer the following questions, giving up to two points for each of the five questions below.

Here's a guide on how to rate your answer:

0	1	2
We are seriously lacking	We're ok here, could be better	Got this one nailed

Is your logo:

a. Clean?	/2
b. Simple (with no more than three elements)?	/2
c. Useable at all sizes (very small to billboard size)?	/2
d. Reflective of your brand promise?	/2
e. Qualitative rating	/2

Total: _____ out of 10

Use the qualitative rating to increase or decrease your score to get what seems "right" on a scale of one to ten. This is a chance to soften your ratings if your score for this element seems too low.

This will give you a rating for this element. Transfer this score to the Launch Elements table on page 158.

Once you have scored all 10 elements in this book, add up the individual scores to get your Launch Readiness Score. These questions are also repeated in the final chapter for your convenience, so you have them all in one place there.

5.

Developing the Website

Your website is your online house. Your home page is the front door of your online house and the other pages store your valuable assets. If you think about your site in this way, you'll be well on your way to providing a good user experience for your site visitors. And you'll also be thinking about your website appropriately in terms of how to invest in it.

Unlike a house, a good website can make you money while you sleep, which is just one of the reasons why you must have a website for your initiative. Although it is less and less common these days, I am still sometimes surprised by companies that come to us and do not have any online presence, or have a weak presence.

Before buyers reach out to a company, they are up to 57% along in their decision to work with that company, according to CEB, a best-practice insight and technology company. How is that possible? Online research.

Make sure your online presence tells the story you want to be telling.

That is how you make money online while you sleep. You never know who is looking at your website and deciding to work with you or simply buying your products 24/7.

First of all, let's consider key questions about building or redesigning your site. Two of the most crucial questions are "Does our website convey our brand story well?" and "Is it quickly and easily clear to people who we are and what we do?"

Failing to get this message across to your visitors is the most common error I see. This is something we work closely with our clients on, ensuring their message is loud and clear, especially on their home page. Time is of the essence online.

According to Chartbeat, a data-analytics company that looked at 2 billion online visits in the course of a month, 55% of site visitors spend fewer than 15 seconds actively on a page. That is about the time it just took you to read the prior sentence.

This Chartbeat data highlights the fact that, while someone may click to view your page, *chances are good they don't read it.* So ... all that time you spent obsessing over the wording in that paragraph on the home page? Wasted. I'm guilty of this as well. As a lover of words, I spend far too much time worrying about how something is phrased.

Much as it pains me I counsel my clients on this obsession with words regularly. Spend much more time on the site's visual design and information architecture (how the information is put together via the navigation and, therefore, the flow through the site that you are designing), and less on the words.

Allocate the time in your redesign to the things that matter most to your visitors. To them, how easy it is to find what they want on the site, the visuals and the "quick messages" are far more important than the sea of words.

Nielson Norman Group, the gold standard for user behavior on the web, supports this argument since their research indicates that users often leave web pages in 10 to 20 seconds. They did, however, have some good news for the word lovers in the crowd because they found that "pages with a clear value proposition can hold people's attention for much longer." But first, let's look at some of the critical visual elements in your site design.

How to Develop Your Information Architecture (Navigation) to Meet the Needs of Your Visitors

In terms of the information architecture (IA), think about what information your typical site visitors want, and then design the IA around them so that the information is quickly accessible. If you sell products online, for example, being able to start shopping is much more important than your "About Us" or "Management Team" pages. If you are an emerging startup, however, your Management Team page is critical to promoting your company as a viable team for investment. If you are a marketing agency, your portfolio or client list may be most important to visitors.

One of the easiest ways to figure out how to match up your information to your visitors' needs is to do a "card sort" exercise. First, make a cue card for each page of your current site (or I use sticky notes on a large flipchart). Put the page title on each card or sticky note and note any special functionality on that page. Yes, there is great software to do this. However, I find the tactile version to be the fastest and most effective way to do this. Then add in any new pages you think are useful. Keep doing that until you run out of page ideas.

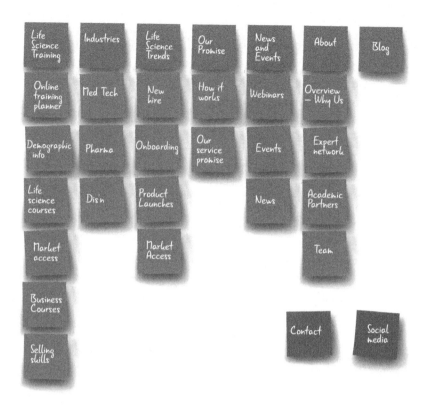

Then arrange the cards on a large table, or your sticky notes onto a flipchart or wall. Rearrange the pages until you have a clear path of information for the most common personas to visit your site. Be sure to note links to other pages (called "contextual links") to lead each persona through your site to relevant content. And, of course, make sure you have clear calls to action for each of your persona profiles on the appropriate pages.

One approach I think is interesting is to have a "New Users Start Here" page. Below is an example from the website ProBlogger. For sites like this that have a lot of content, it's easy to be overwhelmed and just give up on accessing the content. These "Start Here" pages give visitors a quickstart guide to the content.

"Start Here" page to guide users to the best content on common topics

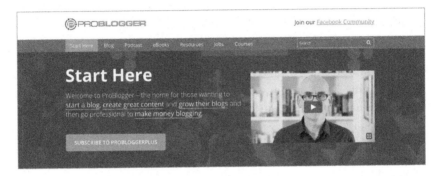

How to Effectively Use Visuals in Web Design

The next thing to consider is whether you are using visuals that support and enhance the key messages that you want to communicate. For example, one of our clients came to us with a well-designed and developed website, except for the main home page image, which was a manufacturing-automation video.

The video was great and visually interesting. However, it gave the impression that the company did something they did not do. (They are a software company, not even in manufacturing.) In that case, the visual did not support their main messages.

When designing a webpage, it's important to step back and look at the Gestalt of your page. By looking at the page title, the visuals and the section subtitles on the page, would someone understand what the page is about? Without reading the text? If so, you've done a great job because that is how most users will experience your page.

While your titles and subtitles are not technically visual, user-experience research shows that the human brain tends to pick up the content in titles and subtitles more often than the full text as we scan over a page. This little bit of neuroscience will help you ensure that your titles and subtitles communicate the key points of your story.

We have a rule at ThinkResults to never waste a subtitle — always use them to reinforce key messages and break up long sections of text. Also, incorporating keyword phrases in your title and subtitles will help with search engine optimization (SEO) for that page, so it's a double bonus. More on SEO later.

Modern Web Design Guidelines

Talking about "modern web design" is like talking about "today's fashions" — it's always changing. As I write this, I suspect the "one-page, multi-section website" (see example below), which has been popular for the last several years, is on its way "out" of fashion. It's been popular because it's great for SEO as all your content is on the home page. It also makes small companies look bigger. It's great for viewing on mobile, which now represents 57% of digital media time online users, according to the 2017 numbers from comScore, a cross-platform measurement company. And we know that number is growing every day.

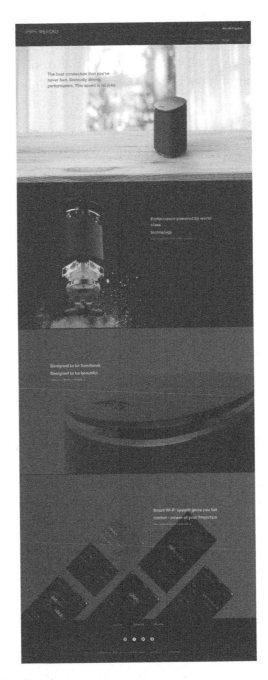

Source: www.Mercku.tech

These are all great reasons to use this popular design format. It has some serious limitations though. First, it's hard to put much content of substance on a single page, unless you want 20 sections or so. Also, if you are serious about SEO, having only one page to optimize limits your options.

Over the years I've been doing web design, I've seen trends come and go. When I first started, having spinning balls as bullets was all the rage (because we could do that and that was cool). We also have tessellated backgrounds (because we hadn't yet figured out how to expand an image well across a page and image options were few … and we were just plain geeky). But now I'm aging myself.

The point is that web design is much like fashion. Maybe not seasonal, but every year or so I see shifts in what we can do on the web, based on new programming languages, and on what people expect as normal in their user experience (note: those expectations go up every year). Now the mix of what is possible (and mostly what is not possible) for mobile users is a huge factor in web design.

As a result, it's important to work with a web designer or agency who is on top of the trends and aware of what is starting to wane. A website is a substantial investment and you don't want your site to be "out" of fashion within the first year of launching it.

Another thing I regularly see are websites that put form before function. This can take any number of faux pas formats, from using Flash (an outdated visual software that renders your site unusable for many users) to not thinking about how the content will work on mobile, and not bothering with simple browser testing so that most people can see your site.

Flash is still popular in the hospitality industry, especially spas and restaurants, because it creates beautiful visuals. However, it's useless on mobile, not SEO friendly, and painful and expensive to update your content.

The second faux pas I see is thinking only in terms of the desktop, or primarily in terms of desktop. The latest data show that 71% of the minutes spent online (in the US) is spent on a mobile device. There is no excuse anymore for not considering the mobile experience.

Designing a site that is mobile first or even mobile friendly requires thinking carefully about many design features. For example, there is no "sidebar" on a mobile screen. Everything flows in a long column, so you must design call-out areas (e.g., customer quotes, calls to action) for mobile, even on your desktop. (The exception, of course, is if you have separate sites for mobile and for desktop. However, having two sites is typically not worth it unless you have a large, complex e-commerce site, like Amazon.)

The third faux pas is not bothering to test on the most popular browsers. This is critical. It's great if you and your client can see the site properly but if half your users don't share the same browser as you two, the site may not render properly for them. Face it, if content is deleted or visuals or formatting messed up, the site could be unreadable or unusable. So what is the point of having a "beautiful" site?

There are several ways to test browsers. One is a browser-simulator program called BrowserStack that you can use to "test" how your site will display on a specific browser. While I love BrowserStack as a filtering tool, I do not recommend relying on it solely.

Unfortunately, many web design agencies, especially offshore contractors, exclusively rely on these software systems. As a result, clients who use these agencies may find that the site that was deemed "ok" on Firefox on a Mac, has all sorts of issues once the site is live. It's not fun to get complaints from a large subsection of your user base when launching a new site. Microsoft Internet Explorer, for example, is famous for requiring "exception coding" to render correctly, and has driven many of my programmers to distraction over the years.

Make sure you know what browsers your audience commonly uses and then ensure the site is tested live (not just software screened) on those major browsers. Your audience may change favorite browsers, and browser use does vary by industry and sector, so ask your web designer for a list of the browsers that the site will be tested on and for which it will be optimized.

Mobile Design Terminology and Guidelines

The terminology used in website design is often confusing even to the pros, so here's a brief overview of some important terms:

Mobile responsive — This site has been designed, typically using a mobile-responsive template from WordPress or other content-management system, to fluidly change its size and the layout of the elements according to the size of the screen it detects. These are the most common type of modern sites on the web right now.

The big benefit is such sites work nicely on small phones, large phones, tablets and desktop monitors of all sizes. One gotcha that often trips people up in these types of sites is that you have ZERO control over things like line breaks and how things are stacked on a page, as those will depend on the size of the user's monitor. So don't waste time and money fussing about how a line breaks in this type of site. Let it go. It's in the hands of the user.

These types of sites are also the hardest to design and test for, since you have to test seemingly endlessly how the elements move fluidly as you change the screen size. The benefit is that, once they are working properly, they will work on ANY size of screen.

Adaptive design — This is an older solution to mobile design, although it makes sense for some large sites like Amazon. In an adaptive design, three different layouts are developed (desktop, tablet and phone), The browser detects which one you are using and serves the appropriate layout up for you. In a complex site like Amazon, this makes sense as people can usually get what they want done with a stripped-down version for the tablet or phone versus the desktop version.

Mobile first — This is a site that has been designed with the mobile user experience as its primary driver. Then the design is "adapted" for desktop. A mobile first site can use either adaptive or responsive design; it's really just a way of thinking. Mobile first is, however, the opposite of how most people think of website design and is the most challenging to do. Mobile design in general is the most restrictive so it really forces the design team to get crystal clear about the purpose of each page. We love doing these kinds of sites, but they are challenging.

No matter which approach or combination of approaches you choose, it's important to understand that mobile design works differently from desktop design. Think about stacking elements as you are designing or working with your designer. When designing for a desktop or large screen, you can line elements up nicely in a row. When viewing that same layout on mobile, those elements will stack one on top of each other so the design will have a different feel to it. Not always a bad thing but certainly something to consider. Make sure your story is still clear when telling it in a vertical, stacked manner.

Here's an example of how a series of elements look on a larger screen.

And then when they are stacked on a tablet or mobile phone.

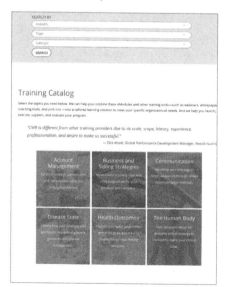

In this case, each tile element stands on its own but clearly the horizontal design could fall apart when stacked vertically. This is where mobile responsive design becomes complex, as there is little control over how elements relate to one another visually. This can get messy fast if you are not experienced at designing for fluid mobile responsive layouts.

Domain Strategy and the Importance of Owning Your Domain Names

One often overlooked part of developing your online presence is your domain strategy — and your defensive domain strategy. The most important factor is that you own a good domain name (or URL — Universal Resource Locator).

The domain name must be your actual name, not some short form, acronym or variation. Variations often lead to brand confusion. If your name is American Paint Supply, be sure to get AmericanPaintSupply.com, not APS.com or AmPaintSupply.com. Otherwise, you will live to regret that choice. At best, it hurts your work to build your brand and costs you money and time. At worst, it hurts your brand, depending on who owns that URL and what the URL is.

Also, you need to secure not only the .com version of your name or .org if you are a nonprofit. You also need to secure the more common variations such as the .co, .net, .org, .com, .info, and so on. Domain names are inexpensive to own and you can redirect anyone who types in your domain name with another extension to your main .com domain.

Also be sure to own common misspellings of your company name as well, such as DieterPaintSupply.com as well as DeiterPaintSupply.com. (Those "e" and "i" reversals will get you every time.) This makes it easy for visitors to find you — even if they are tired and make a mistake when typing in the URL.

An example of a worst case scenario of a defensive domain strategy gone wrong is the Canadian nonprofit, White Ribbon (whiteribbon.com). This group was set up to combat domestic violence after the Montreal Massacre in 1989, where 14 women were killed by a 25-year-old-man who shouted "You're all a bunch of feminists, and I hate feminists!" before opening fire on the students. The White Ribbon movement has since spread to Scotland and Australia.

In 2014, a group called A Voice for Men, designated a hate group by the Southern Poverty Law Center, set up a misleading website on WhiteRibbon. org. The site attempted to delegitimize domestic violence and direct donations toward its own coffers. The site appears to have been taken down now but not before causing a lot of difficulty and cost to the legitimate nonprofit by creating significant brand confusion and potentially losing them critical donations. Learn from mistakes like these. Spend the $10–20 a year for the most common variations of your domain name so you can live peacefully on the web.

By paying attention to the above criteria when building or redesigning your website, you can be sure that you will have an effective online presence. I refer to the name, logo and website as the "Holy Trinity" of launch elements because, together, they really define the new or newly redesigned brand. By the time you get to the website design, you will already have a good name and logo in place, so pay attention to the criteria below to make sure that third element is working as hard as it can for you during your launch.

Website Rating Instructions

Please answer the following questions, giving up to two points for each of the five questions below.

Here's a guide on how to rate your answer:

0	1	2
We are seriously lacking	We're ok here, could be better	Got this one nailed

For your online presence:

a. Do you have a website developed for the initiative?	/2
b. Do you own the actual name as a URL?	/2
c. Have you developed a domain strategy?	/2
d. Does your website tell your brand story well?	/2
e. Qualitative rating	/2

Total: ____ out of 10

Use the qualitative rating to increase or decrease your score to get what seems "right" on a scale of one to ten. This is a chance to soften your ratings if your score for this element seems too low.

This will give you a rating for this element. Transfer this score to the Launch Elements table on page 158.

Note: If you have more than one website for your initiative, average the score across the properties to get a sum out of 10.

Once you have scored all 10 elements in this book, add up the individual scores to get your Launch Readiness Score. These questions are also repeated in the final chapter for your convenience, so you have them all in one place there.

6.

Setting the Sales Strategy

One of the first things I do as a marketing executive when coming into a company is to seek out the head of sales and make him/her my new best friend. Marketing needs to intimately understand what pressures sales are under because we can relieve a lot of their pressures except, of course, those stemming from crappy product design and no market appetite.

As a marketing leader or the company leader, to ensure your launch is successful, you need to evaluate the sales strategy and fix any issues in the sales process. Does the sales team have enough leads? Fix that. Are the leads not the right leads? Fix that. Is the sales team overpromising or selling outside the brand promise? Fix that. You get my point. Most sales problems are marketing problems, so fix them. Align marketing with sales because, without sales, the company is gone.

Making sales happen is the reason marketing exists. It's the reason your company exists. So marketing and sales need to stop bickering. Period.

What is Your Sales Strategy?

One of the most common challenges I see in sales, especially in startups, is that they are trying to sell to everyone. Actually, the sales strategy is often to sell to anyone. That's a problem and it will exhaust the resources of your company. Quickly.

Spreading the sales team too thin also occurs beyond the startup world. A client came to us with lackluster sales after 50 years in business. Recent changes and trends in the marketplace were leaving them poorly positioned via their prior strategy. Through our Launch Assessment process, it became clear that their small sales team was exhausting their resources by trying to be all things to all people. They were pursuing seven different industries with a team of only three people.

Clearly the company needed to get more focused but it wasn't clear which industries would be the best fit. After some detailed market research and analysis of their skills, product and market fit, we refocused their sales strategy on a primary and secondary industry. Shortly thereafter, their sales began to go up, and the sales team's morale and productivity went up significantly as well.

Remember the earlier chapters about the importance of knowing your market when designing a product? Those same rules still apply. I'm not saying that you should turn down opportunistic sales outside your target market. But you should not be spending marketing or sales resources on those sales. Ninety percent of the sales effort should be within your target market. If you cannot sell to the target market that the product has been designed for, you have a much bigger problem than sales.

Develop a clear sales strategy that aligns sales activity with the target market. Start by developing specific persona profiles within the defined target market. This is commonly done by the marketing team. Having these persona profiles in hand will enable the sales team to identify top prospects during their prospecting work. If your sales team is just there to close deals, having these persona profiles at their fingertips allows them to focus on the pains and motivations for the target market persona profiles, which tends to make the sales process easier and faster. If you haven't yet developed ideal persona profiles, go back and read the section on how to do this in the Positioning chapter.

Know Your Lead Process

Once companies know exactly who they are looking for and leads are flowing in nicely, the other problem I frequently see is a lack of process for handling those leads.

A large tech company we worked with had this problem. The marketing campaigns we developed were generating hundreds of highly qualified leads, yet there was no clear process for handling those leads. Or at least the standard company process would take months to implement. With a marketing strategy that was generating new leads every week, waiting months to implement a process to handle the leads clearly was not going to work. To quickly fix the problem, we developed a makeshift lead management process in conjunction with their sales team, keeping them busy with a steady flow of qualified leads.

Before you start marketing, define the process for handling those incoming leads, especially when they are higher than expected. Or at least get with sales and make one up together that works in the short term. You will need to know what will make it easy for your sales team to handle incoming leads and then work within those parameters. Be sure you know the answers to these questions:

- How will leads be collected?

- Are there any restrictions on how they should be handled? (This typically applies more in larger companies with strict privacy rules.)

- How will you pass the relevant leads to sales? Do they want an Excel spreadsheet? Individual emails? Tagging in the CRM system? A weekly review meeting? What do they prefer?

- What will you do with the "net new" leads that sales didn't want? How will you segment and nurture those leads?

- At what point does a nurtured lead get passed back to sales? What is/are the trigger(s)? Is the sales team in alignment with these criteria?

- What does the sales team see as the sticking point right now in sales? How can you fix that?

Once you can answer all these questions, now you are ready to "do" the marketing that will drive leads into sales. Remember, marketing's job is to make the phone ring. The job of sales is to pick up the phone and close the deal. (Thanks, Baer Tierkel, I've never forgotten this nugget you shared years ago as CMO of PeopleSoft.)

Developing the Right Sales Materials

The most important job marketing can do is to make sure the sales team is well armed to answer that ringing phone and to close the deals. This means they need materials at all points of the sales cycle and customer journey.

Although there are many definitions of the sales cycle, this is the most commonly used description and the types of materials the sales team will need at each stage:

1. Prospecting — this is where marketing can be most helpful. At this point, customers need lots of information via your website (Chapter 5) and social media (more in Chapter 8). They will need basic information about who your company is and what it does (on the website/social channels); they will want to read case studies and/or testimonials from other customers, coverage of your company or product in media outlets, guides about how to choose a solution like yours, checklists, online quizzes, ROI calculators, etc.

2. **Setting the appointment** — sales can handle this part on their own, although having guides about how to choose solutions, or online ROI calculators/quizzes to send to the prospect can be a handy tools for sales at this point.

3. **Qualifying** — this will definitely be where those online quizzes and calculators, as well as case studies, can help prospects self-identify as likely consumers of your product or service.

4. **Making your presentation** — clearly this is where marketing can make sure that sales has good, on brand presentation materials that clearly articulate the value of the solution as well as leave behinds and PDFs (such as case studies) to email.

5. **Handling objections** — at this point, the material needed is usually more technical so things like product spec sheets, whitepapers, analyst reports and other detailed materials can be useful here.

6. **Closing** — hopefully this doesn't require marketing ;)

7. **Getting referrals** — it is always wise to remind your sales team to ask a new customer if they have other colleagues who might be interested.

Clearly there is a lot marketing can do to support the sales cycle and customers as they move through their decision process. Case studies are the most useful marketing materials so be sure that you have a program in place to refresh those on a quarterly or monthly basis, depending on your sales volume.

Why are case studies so valuable? First, they have the weight of a third party discussing how your solution helped them. Second, they describe a real-world problem, not some vague marketing speak. Third, they allow prospects to connect with the other company's problems and gain some insight or at least a sense of shared experience with the problem. This gives you an advantage because it's now clear that the problem is external to the company and it's solvable. That gives hope and a shared enemy: the problem can be solved — by using your company's solution.

Providing great content at all points of the sales cycles removes friction for both the customer and the sales person. This ensures that the process flows smoother, and helps assure your company's success.

Training the Sales Force

Once you have defined your sales strategy, have a lead-management process in place and materials at all points of the sales cycle, you're done, right? Not quite yet. Now it's time to make sure your sales team knows what to do with all those new sales tools. Have you trained them on the new positioning? Do they know the details of your target markets and personas? Do they know how to communicate the benefits of those great features in the product to those prospects?

If not, it's time to set up sales training. Don't assume that your sales team will "just figure it out." Set up training and have a regular schedule of training to keep them updated as the product changes.

This can be as simple as a one-hour conference call with a brief PowerPoint presentation or demo and your marketing person, or you can develop more detailed online training that the sales team can use in bits and pieces. Make it easy for them to digest the information in small sections at a time. Micro-training is much easier for an active salesperson to do and learn from than taking one or two days out of their schedule to sit and learn.

The key point is to make the training easy for you to develop and for salespeople to absorb so that you can do it continuously. Your company is constantly changing and evolving. Make sure you are bringing the sales team along with those changes.

Staying in Touch with Sales

One final note on sales strategy and processes. Be sure to have regular communications with sales on how things are going.

Not only do you want feedback from sales on how the marketing programs are working (are they getting enough of the right kinds of leads?), you also want to hear from them what customers and prospects are saying. This feedback is extremely valuable. It's free market research basically.

Let sales tell you what it is about the product that people understand and don't understand. What are the concerns, objections and additional features they want to see?

We recently went through this process with a large tech company as we were planning the next generation of the product. It was helpful to see that most of the requests from customers about they wanted in the next-gen product were already designed into the new version. We also identified some gaps for the product team to figure out how to fill via updates or later in the product roadmap.

In summary, by making sure your sales strategy is clearly defined, with processes for handling incoming leads, for updating and delivering new sales materials, and for ensuring your sales team is trained on the new materials, you will be in a strong position to launch your product, service or company. Remember, sales is the bedrock of your company. If sales isn't working, nothing else will. Sales cure everything.

Sales Strategy Rating Instructions

Please answer the following questions, giving up to two points for each of the five questions below.

Here's a guide on how to rate your answers:

0	1	2
We are seriously lacking	We're ok here, could be better	Got this one nailed

Do you have:

a. A defined sales strategy?	/2
b. A process for handling incoming leads?	/2
c. Consistent sales materials?	/2
d. Sales tools and training?	/2
e. Qualitative rating	/2

Total: ____ out of 10

Use the qualitative rating to increase or decrease your score to get what seems "right" on a scale of one to ten. This is a chance to soften your ratings if your score for this element seems too low.

This will give you a rating for this element. Transfer this score to the Launch Elements table on page 158.

Once you have scored all 10 elements in this book, add up the individual scores to get your Launch Readiness Score. These questions are also repeated in the final chapter for your convenience, so you have them all in one place there.

7.

Crafting the Content Strategy

Content marketing has been growing in importance over the last decade and today is threatening the role of traditional and even digital advertising. This is particularly true in business to business (B2B) marketing. With 67% of the buying decision being done digitally, the role of content cannot be denied.

So how do you "do" content marketing? Here are some questions to consider.

Do You Have a Mix of Content Types That Can Be Delivered at Various Points Across the Sales Cycle?

As we discussed in the chapter on sales strategy, you must have a mix of content and content in different formats along the customer journey. Earlier in the buyer journey, that content must be buyer education pieces. Think about what kinds of content can help your prospects learn more about your company, your solution and the benefits your solution can bring.

At this stage, buying guides, and interactive content such ROI calculators and quizzes can help buyers. Such formats help buyers think about how they would choose among the various offerings in your industry. You want to move them from awareness into consideration. The key is to get them thinking about choosing *any* solution. Often your biggest obstacle is the law of inertia. People at rest tend to stay at rest. They tend not to buy any solution at all, yours or your competitor's.

Later in the buyer journey, it becomes more important to provide content that helps them validate the decision to choose *your* solution. Content such as checklists (to make sure the prospect is thinking about the right features in a potential product or service), case studies that are relevant to their industry, whitepapers and technical specs documents they can hand to their technical teams if they are influencing the decision, become important here.

You will also need different kinds of content for different channels. What you tweet, for example, is vastly different than the content you deliver from the podium of a major conference.

Think about how you can create great experiences for the readers, listeners and viewers of the various forms of your content. What is the experience of a large-scale keynote talk from your company executive? What is the experience when the salespeople do their first pitch to a customer? What is the experience created from the SlideShare deck you're posting? How about the experience of reading your latest blog posts? Right down to every tweet, a different experience of your company is created with every post. Use that time wisely.

Another consideration in your content strategy is how will you engage different learning styles as prospects seek to learn more about your company. Not all of us are linguistically dominant learners, those who best take in information from words. There are seven learning styles in all, and each has preferences that should be considered when developing a spectrum of content:

- Visual (spatial) — These learners understand concepts better through visual information such as pictures, images and spatial relations.

- Aural (auditory-musical) — These folks learn better through sound and music.

- Verbal (linguistic) — These learners prefer using both written and spoken words to learn.

- Physical (kinesthetic) — These people do better when they can use their bodies and hands to learn something, activating their sense of touch.

- Logical (mathematical) — These folks want to learn through logic, reasoning and systems.

- Social (interpersonal) — These learners prefer to learn in group settings.

- Solitary (intrapersonal) — These learners prefer to work alone and do better when they can study the material themselves.

Of course, each person has a blend of learning styles, and will often have one or two more dominant styles. The more you can integrate different elements into your content, the more people you will be able to engage, and the more of your material they will be able to integrate.

It may not be possible to integrate different elements into your content in all formats (e.g., tweet), but it is certainly possible in longer formats such as conference talks and workshops. Plan for a variety of exercises, for example, that address the needs of solitary learners as well as social learners. For example, when I'm doing a talk, I often include an exercise early on that asks listeners to write down their intentions, ideas and thoughts related to the subject we are discussing. This allows everyone to participate early on, and sets it up quickly so that the audience understands that the presentation will not be a sit-back-and-take-notes kind of talk.

These exercises also allow solitary learners a chance to gather their thoughts and also engage the skills of logical, kinesthetic and verbal learners. Then I usually move into one or two group exercises to engage the social and aural learners, while still including the verbal and the kinesthetic learners.

Graphics and props keep the visual learners engaged throughout, and having a strong structure and facts to back up my points engages the logical learners again.

As you can see, with just a little thinking, it's simple to create content that engages all seven types of learners. This process can also be followed when writing content such as whitepapers. It's true that it's a bit harder to engage the physical, aural and social learners, but even they can be included with creative exercises or links to resources that will appeal to their needs. Podcasts, for example, are a great way to engage the aural learners, and can be fantastic for engaging executives who often travel a lot, time where they can easily be listening to your content.

Repurposing: How to Create 50+ Pieces of Content

Content creation can be hard work, especially long-form content such as whitepapers, podium presentations, keynotes and books.

The good news is once you have created this main thought leadership piece of content, it's a snap to create 50 or more pieces of content to be used across a variety of channels that will appeal to a range of learning styles. How, you ask?

Let's use a whitepaper as an example. From the content in a typical whitepaper, the following 50+ pieces of content can be derived:

- 4 blog posts on your website
- 4 blog posts on LinkedIn
- 12 tweets
- 12 Facebook posts
- 12 updates on LinkedIn
- 2–3 infographics

- 1 webcast

- 1 podium presentation

- 1 SlideShare deck

- 4 videos

- 1 trend report

- 1 executive highlights report

  Total: 55–56 pieces of content

For the most part, these various forms of "new" content are simple derivations of the original content, and some of these will require repackaging of the content. Pretty easy, right? The best part is that it means you don't have to come up with "new" content all the time, which can be draining. Repurposing content also means your message will be consistent and people are more likely to see it than if it was just a one-and-done posting.

Earned, Owned and Paid Content: Why You Need All of Them

In the world of content marketing, there are three broad categories or types of content. You need some of each in your content strategy. Let's start with "earned" content.

Earned

This is typically content such as articles written by third parties and generally follows sustained public relations efforts by your team or outside agency. This type of content is extremely valuable, especially when you are launching a startup. Earned content gives your company exposure to a larger audience and that crucial third-party validation. This kind of content has more credibility than the user-generated type, because everyone knows you don't control the final product.

So how do you go about "earning" content? With a smart public relations (PR) strategy, of course. This typically will include four major elements: identifying your target media, developing your story, getting references and generating reviews. Let's look at each element separately.

Identifying Your Target Media

The first step in a good PR strategy is to research and define your target list of publications, reporters and key influencers. Everyone wants to be in *The Wall Street Journal* or *The New York Times*. But there is an unwritten rule in the PR world. National publications will rarely write about a company that has not yet been covered in local and regional publications. And this is definitely true for national television or radio. They do NOT want an unproven guest on their show. So while you will want to know where you eventually want to be in terms of key publications, you will need to start with your local media to get there. Hint: start now ....

Developing Your Main Story

The second step is to develop your main story, which will become your news release for launch. These have specific formats that reporters understand so be sure to engage a professional for this. You may have multiple news releases over time but generally there is just one for the current launch. A word to the wise regarding wire services for distribution: don't use a "free" wire service. You get what you pay for in PR.

Developing Key Customers to Speak on Your Behalf as References

Reporters will ask for customer references so make sure you have two to three lined up before you do outreach to reporters. Things can happen blazingly fast in the PR world and you want to be sure you can quickly offer a reporter a customer who has agreed to be a reference, has been properly prepped by your PR team, and understands your positioning and messaging (see Chapter 3).

Reviews from Key Influencers

More and more it's important to have good reviews from credible sources at the time of launch. You need to arrange this advance to make sure the reviews hit at launch. You may need to send samples to key influencers before the launch and "pitch" them on why their readers or viewers would be interested in this product. Or perhaps you need Amazon reviews to be up within the first few days of launch? Leave adequate time for your reviewers to complete these tasks. I like to give them samples of reviews to make it easy for them to emphasize the key points we want reinforced. This is where the positioning work outlined in Chapter 3 becomes exceedingly handy.

This third-party validation is why so many startups have the "As Featured In" running across their websites so prominently. Google also loves placements in prestigious traditional media, raising your search engine optimization (SEO).

Prominent feature of press coverage (TVision Insights, a Microsoft Accelerator portfolio company)

One final note about earned media. Speed is the name of the game here. I warn my execs that, yes, we can get you great coverage but you will have to drop what you are doing when a reporter calls and answer their questions. Reporters typically need answers within a few hours of contacting you.

I've had execs get huffy about this as they are not accustomed to rearranging their day. I remind them that we discussed the likelihood that this would happen and do they want to get that *The Wall Street Journal* article? This is what "earned" media means – you typically have little control over when or how it happens. Be prepared, be open, and be quick in your responses. A good article in a key publication can last over many years of a product's life or even over your career. It's worth it.

Owned

The second major category of content is owned content, material you generate yourself, such as your website, blogs, social media posts, email newsletters, whitepapers, webinars, presentations, and collateral.

I would argue this is the most important form of content because it is your intellectual property and you have 100% control over it. As social media channels turn more and more to monetization models that suppress content from folks other than their big advertisers, it can be harder and harder to get your message out via other organization's channels.

Owning your own content and your own distribution network is critical to maintaining an ongoing relationship with your customers, prospects and the greater community (more on this in the email marketing section below).

Paid

The final type of content is, quite simply, advertising. Essentially, it is any paid promotional materials, whether it's Google AdWords, display advertising, Facebook advertising, website and email newsletter ads, or even traditional print ads. You have 100% control over the message, since you pay for that privilege.

Digital advertising is more and more a part of the overall marketing mix and it can be easy to get started on say, Google AdWords or Facebook, with relatively small budgets. The real beauty of digital ads is everything is measured so it's easy to figure out where to put more money and where to put less to maximize your results.

The challenge is it can take quite a bit of time and expertise to optimize these channels. For example, I spoke with a company that was spending more than $1M a year on Facebook ads. While they were seeing revenue return for this investment, they had not yet broken even, let alone seen any profit from the campaign, which had gone on for more than a year. The marketing leader was convinced it was just a matter of figuring out how to optimize the Facebook ad code, despite having a dedicated Facebook account manager. I suspected that they needed a more integrated marketing mix, but they were committed to more digital ad spending.

Digital advertising is like snowboarding. Easy to learn, hard to master. Beware of "trying" to do everything through digital advertising. Make sure it's just one part of your content mix.

Is Your Content Engaging, Drawing People to Your Brand?

While developing lots of new content across all three content types is a great approach, it's much better to develop the minimal amount of content needed to create the most engagement possible. Be lazy in your content development. That, to me, is the holy grail of content marketing. How is this possible? By increasing the engagement level of each piece.

Other than adding kittens to your video (a guaranteed way to make your content go viral), there are two major trends that can help you consistently make your content engaging.

Current Trends in Content Marketing

Two big trends in content marketing are more visual content and more user-generated content.

Visual content, such as infographics, photos, diagrams, charts, and even video, is not likely to go away. Today even the average person can create attractive visuals and even videos. The old adage about a picture being worth a thousand words is as true today as it ever was. With a barrage of content coming at us every day, being able to absorb that information visually makes it easier on our brains.

Images are processed 60,000 thousand times faster than text. Think about that for a second. Research from MIT indicates that the human brain can process an image that is only seen for as little 13 milliseconds. Twitter research shows that adding a picture to your post will increase the likelihood of a retweet by 35%, more than any other piece of content, including videos. So yes, use neuroscience to your advantage and add more visual content to your mix — it is proven to increase engagement, making your content more effective.

Photo posts garner more engagement than any other kind of post, including video posts

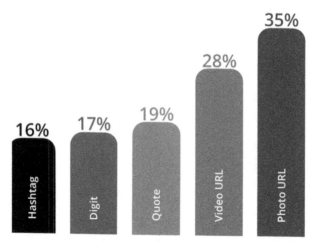

Source:http://www.socialmediaexaminer.com/wp-content/uploads/2014/05/pr-photo-retweets.png

User-generated Content Fuels Engagement

User-generated content is not likely to go away anytime for two simple reasons. It makes content generation easier for companies, and it engages your community in a fun way.

One example I love BarkBox, a monthly subscription of treats and toys that gets delivered to us (for our Golden Retriever) each month. Each month has a theme and often there's a prop (think photo booth props for dogs) as part of the box, encouraging us to snap a picture of our dog and the prop and post it on social media. BarkBox typically receives hundreds of submissions, generating a lot of traffic on their social media feeds and free content for them to use to promote their brand.

User-generated images on #BarkBoxDay, the day the monthly subscription of toys and treats arrives for subscribers.

What Is BarkBox?   Monthly Themes   **BARK·BOX**   💬 Chat   Login   Get Started

Pups Who Ruv It
See why #BarkBoxDay drives pups bonkers!

How can you create a campaign that invites users to upload and share their content (especially visuals)? It's a great way to involve and connect the members of your community, and increase engagement in the process.

Focus on Your Customer First: WIIFM

However, make sure your content focuses on the customer, not on you. This is commonly known in the marketing world as "WIIFM" — "What's In It for Me?"

When I was heading up communications for a division of PeopleSoft, if the draft of a document started with the word "PeopleSoft," I sent it back to the writer for a re-write. I made my writers mad by doing this but, to be fair, I had explained my thinking and how I wanted case studies, whitepapers and other collateral to be set up, which is as follows:

- First, put yourself in the shoes of the person reading the document — what is in it for them? What is their biggest concern? What pains are they currently experiencing that your solution can relieve or eliminate? Make sure that first paragraph is about their experience, demonstrating that you understand their predicament and challenges. This is an act of simple respect.

- Once you have fully explored their predicament and made it clear that you understand their pain, then — and only then — can you start a sentence with "<my company> provides <specific solution> designed to address <your pains>." And proceed to explain the benefits of your company's solution.

This philosophy of developing content is a simple translation into business communications of the enduring Stephen Covey Rule #5: Seek first to understand, then to be understood. Bringing humanity and compassion to your content will serve both you and your customers well.

Focus on Benefits to Your Customer: A Trend That Will Never Get Old

We love to talk about what we call "feeds and speeds" in tech marketing, describing in graphic detail the technical details and whiz-bang features of our latest product. Rarely does the material bother to explain the value of those features, in other words the benefit for the customer. Technology is only great when it solves a problem.

Let's look at a real-life example from a major tech company. In the example below, the feature being highlighted on the left is that the new product has an "integrated hardware (HW) and software (SW) package and design." Cool. So what does that do for me? That's the benefit we are looking for, which is on the right.

Since the product has the hardware/software integration already built in, the product is easier for developers to just plug it in and start developing ("more plug-and-play"). So the business benefit is you should be able to get the product to market faster since your developers don't need to mess around with integration issues.

Moving a feature into business benefit language

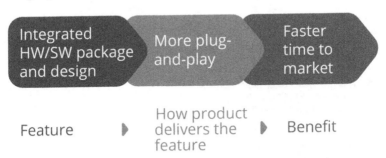

Focusing on the business benefits is much more compelling to the folks writing the checks than focusing on the technical details of how that benefit is achieved. If you have developed any trust in your brand over the years, customers will expect that you have the whiz bang tech to make things happen. Again, highlighting business benefits is a way of focusing on the customer and how you will help them. Focusing on the features is a way of focusing on you and how cool you are. Don't go there.

Long Live the Red-headed Stepchild of Content Marketing: Email Marketing

"Email marketing is dead." Over the years, I've heard that statement so many times. And every time, the experts were wrong.

Yes, we all hate email. Yet it is a primary communication tool, especially for business users. And study after study shows that email performs consistently higher than any other form of content marketing. Why? Because it's a direct conversation with your community.

For example, a 2016 study by the Content Marketing Institute and Marketing Profs found that business-to-business marketers cited email as the number one reason (91%) for their success in content marketing.

Email cited as the top driver in overall content marketing success

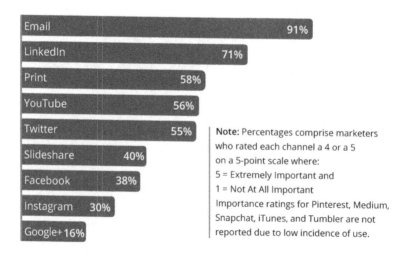

Email — 91%
LinkedIn — 71%
Print — 58%
YouTube — 56%
Twitter — 55%
Slideshare — 40%
Facebook — 38%
Instagram — 30%
Google+ — 16%

Note: Percentages comprise marketers who rated each channel a 4 or a 5 on a 5-point scale where: 5 = Extremely Important and 1 = Not At All Important Importance ratings for Pinterest, Medium, Snapchat, iTunes, and Tumbler are not reported due to low incidence of use.

Source: http://contentmarketinginstitute.com/wp-content/uploads/2016/12/b2b-content-marketing-2017-benchmarks-budgets-trends-north-america-600x402.jpg

Everyone who has given you their email wants to stay in touch with your company and wants to receive information from you. That is known as permission marketing, a term coined by Seth Godin. These people have given you their permission to market to them. This is the most sacred and valuable form of marketing. Use it wisely and use it well. Email is nowhere near dead.

Do You have a Strategy for Consistently Delivering Your Content?

One final note on content marketing. While developing great content is an excellent place to focus, the most important thing to remember is that consistency matters. From both a customer expectation perspective and search engine optimization considerations, being regular in your communications is the key to unlocking your content marketing success.

From a customer perspective, people need to hear from you regularly or they will forget about you. Sounds harsh but it's true. I recently experienced this firsthand as I wanted to call a writer I knew would be perfect for a project but could not remember her name. I hadn't heard from her at all in several years. I never did remember her name and hired someone else to do the work.

Whether your content is delivered via a monthly newsletter (I highly recommend this strategy), daily social posts, or even a weekly note (a colleague of mine does this effectively), choose a schedule and commit your resources. Those resources can be you, or someone you hire to make sure it gets done regularly. Many clients use ThinkResults to ensure they are communicating with customers on a regular basis, knowing they just don't have the time to be consistent about it.

An added bonus for regular communications, at least on your website via your blog for example, is that the search engine bots will get "trained" that you post every Thursday at 10 am. Over time, the bots will be programmed to check your site for new content at your regularly scheduled time. This means your content will get indexed and promoted via search to potential customers much faster than if you posted on an irregular basis. A nice added benefit for you.

In summary, content marketing plays a crucial role in the launch of your product, company, or service. Be sure you have a mix of content types, ideally for different learner types, and content that can be delivered at all points of the sales cycle. Also make sure you have a strategy for consistently delivering great content to your customers and prospects. Executing these strategies well means that it will be easy for customers and prospects to buy from you, which is the purpose of any business.

Content Strategy Rating Instructions

Please answer the following questions, giving up to two points for each of the five questions below.

Here's a guide on how to rate your answer:

0	1	2
We are seriously lacking	We're ok here, could be better	Got this one nailed

Do you have:

a. A mix of content types?	/2
b. Content that can be delivered at various points in the sales cycle?	/2
c. Engaging content that draws people to your brand?	/2
d. A strategy for delivering content appropriately?	/2
e. Qualitative rating	/2

Total: ___ out of 10

Use the qualitative rating to increase or decrease your score to get what seems "right" on a scale of one to ten. This is a chance to soften your ratings if your score for this element seems too low.

This will give you a rating for this element. Transfer this score to the Launch Elements table on page 158.

Once you have scored all 10 elements in this book, add up the individual scores to get your Launch Readiness Score. These questions are also repeated in the final chapter for your convenience, so you have them all in one place there.

8.

Setting the Social Strategy

The most common problem I find with social media strategies is that they generally seem to consist of "Let's cover as many channels as we can, inconsistently, and see what happens." As the saying goes, hope is not a strategy.

Your social media strategy for launch and beyond needs to focus on those channels that will bring you the most impact, with the least effort. If you haven't noticed this about me, I am focused on efficiency. Marketing to me is not about spending money. It's about leveraging time and money for maximum market impact. The same is true with social media, which can be a huge drain on your time, or an efficient driver of growth for your company. The difference lies in your strategy and approach.

One of the most interesting facets of social media marketing is that it is not a monolith. There is no "social media." There are only a collection of social media channels. Each has its own unique personality and strength. We will dig into each of today's most popular channels and their personalities soon, so you can decide which one (or handful of them) makes the most sense for your launch and ongoing marketing strategy.

Speaking of channels, I will warn you, as I warn all our clients, about getting high and mighty about Facebook. "We can't be on there; that's for personal stuff." Really? You mean that none of the 2.07 billion monthly active users on Facebook might be prospects for your business? I know, you want to be on LinkedIn, but as a marketer, I say go where the eyeballs and the engagement are.

While I love LinkedIn and think every business should be on there, you are much more likely to get better engagement, even with a serious B2B company, on Facebook. Don't miss out on the chance to be in front of those 2.07 billion active users every month.

But back to figuring out which channels are best for you. Although there is a lot of chatter about the various channels, it's important to have perspective about the real players in the social media landscape:

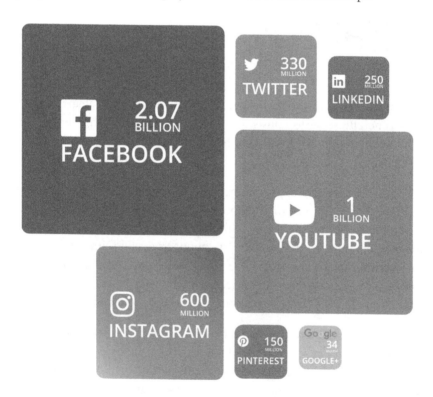

The big players consistently are Facebook, by far the largest, and then YouTube. Then for business users, the smaller but most useful networks are Instagram, Twitter, Pinterest, LinkedIn and Google+. While these numbers are changing and shifting somewhat over time (this data is from November 2017), this gives you a sense of the real behemoths in social media.

Here's a brief rundown of the major social media channels in order of size. (And yes, new ones crop up every day, and the data is changing over time, but focus on the numbers of users — that's where your impact is.)

Facebook

The granddaddy of social media networks

- Facebook has 2.07B monthly active users. (Except for YouTube, all the other top channels are in the millions.)

- 510,000 comments are posted per minute.

- The average time spent per Facebook visit is 20 minutes.

- 50% of 18- to 24-year-olds go on Facebook when they wake up.

- 76% of women and 66% of men who go online visit Facebook.

Stats — https://zephoria.com/top-15-valuable-facebook-statistics/

Source: http://www.socialmediatoday.com/social-networks/top-social-network-demographics-2017-infographic

YouTube

Second largest search engine in the world (behind Google)

- YouTube has 1 billion users.

- 82% of online content will be delivered by video by 2020, according to estimations by Cisco.

- Searches for "how-to" videos on YouTube are growing 70% year over year.

- 80% of 18- to 49-year-olds watch YouTube in an average month.

- YouTube reaches more 18- to 49-year-olds than any U.S cable network.

Source: http://www.socialmediatoday.com/social-networks/top-social-network-demographics-2017-infographic

Instagram

The fastest growing network

- Instagram has 600 million monthly users.

- 59% of them are between the ages of 18 and 29.

- 70% of posts are not seen.

- More than 70% of businesses are using Instagram.

- Posts with at least one hashtag average 12.6% more engagement.

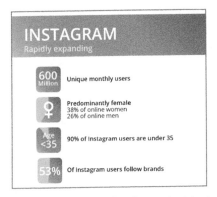

Source: http://www.socialmediatoday.com/social-networks/top-social-network-demographics-2017-infographic

Stats: https://www.smartinsights.com/social-media-marketing/instagram-marketing/instagram-statistics/

Twitter

Great for news and finding reporters

- Twitter has 330 million monthly active users.

- Almost one quarter (24.6%) of the accounts belong to journalists.

- The most common age demographic is between 18 to 29 years old, representing 35% of users.

- 45% of Twitter's news users are college graduates.

- 30% of online Americans who earn $75,000 or more visit Twitter.

- 69% of users have made a purchase from a small or medium-sized business because of something they saw on Twitter.

- 44% of users have never posted a tweet. "Only" 550 million have ever posted a tweet.

- 80% access Twitter via mobile.

- Using an image results in 18% more click throughs, 89% more likes, and 150% more retweets.

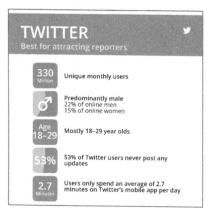

Source: http://www.socialmediatoday.com/social-networks/top-social-network-demographics-2017-infographic

LinkedIn

Prime channel for B2B companies

- LinkedIn has 250 million monthly users.

- 44% of users make more than $75,000 a year.

- 40% of LinkedIn users visit it daily.

- The channel is adding two new members every second.

- 13% of LinkedIn users do not have a Facebook account.

- 59% of LinkedIn users don't use Twitter.

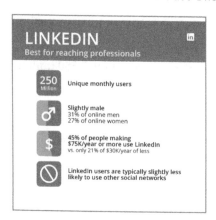

Source: http://www.socialmediatoday.com/social-networks/top-social-network-demographics-2017-infographic

Pinterest

The visual arts

- Pinterest has more than 150 million monthly active users (up from 100 million in 2015).

- Pinterest went after more male users in 2015 and they now account for 40% of new signups.

- 87% of Pinners have purchased a product because of Pinterest.

- 83% of Pinterest users would rather follow a brand than a celebrity.

- Active Pinners have a 9% higher average income than non-users.

Source: http://www.socialmediatoday.com/social-networks/top-social-network-demographics-2017-infographic

Google+

Fantastic for search engine optimization (SEO)

- Google+ has 34 million unique monthly visits.

- Since Google controls search, having a presence on Google+ will help your search engine rankings, making it easier for your business to be found.

- As of 2016, 91% of Google+ accounts were empty.

I do not recommend spending much time on original content for Google+. Most Google accounts are created to access other Google services or are bot/spam accounts. However, Google owns search so having content on Google+ gives you great SEO value. According to Buffer, a popular social-media-management platform, "content that you post to Google+ is far more likely to show up in search results than other pages, websites, articles, and content posted to other social networks because Google ranks its own social network higher and crawls it faster. The added benefit is that Google even previews certain Google+ posts with rich snippets (e.g., profile picture, media), giving them even more real estate in a search."

So you should definitely post content on Google+ for SEO reasons. Just don't expect to create a community there.

A Word On Snapchat

Snapchat appears to be dying a slow death, so a far better option for companies is the Instagram Stories feature. It is essentially the same thing as Snapchat, but it's much easier to build a following on Instagram. According to MediaKix, an influencer-marketing agency, Instagram Stories stalled Snapchat's user growth by 82% and top influencers appear to be leaving Snapchat for Instagram.

Take a close look at each of the channels and think about which one to three of the channels are the best match for your business, your audience and your content. Are you primarily targeting females with visual content? Then you should be on Pinterest as well as on Facebook. Do you want to reach reporters? Then Twitter should be in your top channels. Are millennials your prime target? Then make sure Instagram is in your top three channels. Making sure you are matching the personality of each channel to what you want to accomplish will get you out of the "but I love Snapchat" discussion and on the road to social-media-marketing success.

Question: Do You Have a Strategy for Filling the Channels With Ongoing Content?

Once you have figured out which your best channels are, the next big question is what is your strategy for filling the channels with relevant and ongoing content. As we discussed in Chapter 7 (Content Strategy), ensuring you have a regular cadence of material is critical for social media channels.

Social media is a fantastic opportunity for you to engage with your extended community on a regular and ongoing basis — for free. It's a marketing dream. That does not mean, however, that you now have license to promote your company nonstop.

One of the best ways to ensure you always have the right content for your social media channels is to set up an editorial calendar. There may be certain national holidays, major trade conferences or awareness days or months that are relevant to your company. Making sure you have relevant posts will help prevent last-minute scrambles for those events and ensures you don't miss them altogether either.

In addition to the relevant monthly or yearly events, it's helpful to have at least a loose schedule of topic areas you want to cover every week. This ensures that you have an even balance of topics over time.

For example, at ThinkResults, we try to make sure that we have an inspirational quote and image to kick off the week on Mondays, a post on startups/entrepreneurs, one on productivity or how to be a more effective leader at work during the week, and a funny marketing joke or comic to end the week on Fridays. That leaves us with one day a week of open topics to cover things like upcoming speaking events, promoting various events from relevant professional organizations, and sharing client news.

For the most part, our content is focused on our audience who are startups and change agents inside large corporations. About 10–20% of our content is focused on promoting our company or me directly. That's about the right ratio. About 80% of your content should be inspiring, funny or otherwise useful to your community, depending on your brand.

In contrast, several years ago, a large international beverage company was implementing a self-centered social media campaign that involved images of their product in all different kinds of settings. Clearly that was not successful as they completely changed their strategy a few months later to a much more interesting and engaging campaign. The company shall remain unnamed.

On the other hand, a small Bay Area nonprofit, Operation Freedom Paws (OFP), of which I am now a Board member and have been advising them informally for several years, has a much more interesting and engaging strategy for their social media channels. I introduced the organization earlier in the Logo chapter of this book.

Although we did advise them on their original social media strategy which increased their fans 10x from 800 followers to almost 8,000, they brilliantly devised the following editorial calendar all on their own. To date, their Facebook community remains a very active part of their extended community, pushing out the OFP experience from their Canine Education Center into the virtual world with their Facebook fans around the world on a daily basis.

Here is their social media editorial calendar:

- Monday — Mentoring Mondays, this is a great day to get training and dog care tips from the Executive Director, Mary Cortani, an Army K9 trainer, or one of her mentor trainers

- Tuesday — Tuesday Triumphs, the day to share recent successes someone in the community has had with their dog, or in their lives

- Wednesday — Wordless Wednesday is photo day, "hopefully cute!" as they say

- Thursday — Thursday Thank You is a short bio or story about one of the dogs, supporters, students, etc.

- Friday — Friday Philosophy Day is usually a great picture with a fun quote or training philosophy, or inspiring quote about life with dogs

This calendar provides clear structure and gives fans days to look forward to certain topics. I'm always watching Mondays, for example, for training tips I can use with my rambunctious young Golden Retriever. Wordless Wednesday is also popular as their volunteer professional photographers take the most gorgeous photos of the dogs and their handlers in training class.

This strategy allows OFP to share the executive director's extensive expertise in dog training, show off some fun photos, and share the stories of the people and organizations that are part of their ecosystem to support the vets and the dogs. And as one of the site's administrators, I can tell you that Wordless Wednesdays are popular as are the Thursday Thank You posts that call out key supporters.

Why does this work? Because OFP is delivering quality, engaging content on topics that matter to their fans. This is the heart of any good content marketing strategy. You don't have to be big to be smart about social.

Question: Do You Have a Strategy for Engaging With Your Target Audiences on Those Channels?

Once you've figured out which social media channels are best for your organization and have developed a good following, the next natural evolution will be "how can I engage more with our community on Facebook/Twitter/Instagram/LinkedIn/whatever is your best channel"?

Part of that answer is how you got all those great followers to begin with and part of it is more complicated. You got those thousands or tens of thousands of followers by providing them with great content. Engaging them with content means understanding what motivates them to take action, which may be specific to your organization or community.

There are some known best practices in social media. For example, Facebook content tends to do best when it's fun, positive and uplifting. Most people use Facebook as a break from work, a distraction from their daily lives, so positive, funny and inspiring content, especially visual content, tends to do well. That's why cat videos are so popular.

The other factor that drives engagement, especially on short-lived content channels such as Twitter, is volume. The more you post, especially on Twitter, the more engagement with your content you are likely to see. You literally cannot post too much on Twitter. The half-life of a tweet (the length of time before it's essentially gone to most users) is about 15 minutes. Meaning you can literally post every 15 minutes on Twitter and people still may not see all your posts. (And do you want followers who have so little to do that they catch your every post on Twitter?)

Both LinkedIn and Facebook tend to have longer half-lives, about three to four hours. As a result, posting one to two times in the day is usually best on these channels. I once live posted every 15 minutes from a Microsoft pitch event onto my Facebook feed. (Each company had 10 minutes to pitch.) My friends thought I had lost my mind and/or someone had taken over my phone because I was posting "too much." I was just super excited to see all the companies I had been mentoring doing their pitches to the investors gathered at this live event, and wanted to give them all some extra exposure. But I learned my lesson about "over-posting" on Facebook.

Case Study:
How We Drove Triple-digit Increases in Social Media Reach and Engagement on Facebook, Twitter and LinkedIn

One of our clients, Lazarex Cancer Foundation, is a nonprofit that improves patient access to cancer clinical trials. The organization was having some success with their social media but wanted it to be a much stronger part of their marketing mix. Before working with us, social media was a part-time focus for the communications director. It was among many other priorities on her daily list and she knew it wasn't getting the attention it deserved. The organization had a good following on Facebook (about 9,000 followers) and lots of high-quality content for us to use.

We knew that we could increase the performance of their social media program starting with the foundation they had built, then developing a more focused social media strategy optimized through detailed analysis of their web and social metrics.

After just three months of working with the ThinkResults team and implementing the new social media strategy, the Lazarex social metrics began to skyrocket. Here are the results that we saw:

- 29% increase in web traffic, including a 137% increase in the number of users coming to the website from social channels

- 288% increase in reach on Facebook

- 200% increase in engagement on Facebook

- 553% increase in reach on Twitter

So how did we achieve that kind of triple-digit growth in just 90 days? By focusing on clean execution of a clear and compelling social media strategy. We figured out what kind of content was most engaging to people and when they typically engaged with the content. Then we set up a plan to deliver the content they wanted when they wanted it. It really is that simple. Implementation, of course, is where the details live.

We began by doing an audit of all the social media channels Lazarex was trying to cover (I think it was nine) and the type of content and followers they had on each. We discussed what they were trying to achieve and developed the following social media channel strategy:

1. Facebook would be their primary channel, since they had a good following there and were already seeing some engagement by the community. In terms of metrics, we focused primarily on engagement (e.g., likes, shares, comments).

2. **Twitter** growth would be the second priority, since they wanted to attract media attention and influencers. For metrics, we focused on overall growth numbers (e.g., followers, impressions) and tracked new influencers we picked up as part of our "smart following" campaign.

3. **LinkedIn** would be the third priority, since we wanted to garner attention from the pharmaceutical industry. Here we looked at all the metrics in terms of growth and engagement and specifically whether key influencers were interacting with the content and what type of content was the most engaging. LinkedIn was a good place to do outreach to the pharmaceutical industry as Lazarex enables more equitable patient access to pharma's clinical trials.

For the remaining channels (Pinterest, Instagram, Google+, YouTube) we designated an opportunistic strategy that would address content there. For example, any good visual content would be posted on Pinterest and Instagram. Good new videos would be published on YouTube and cross-promoted on Facebook, LinkedIn and Twitter. So Facebook posts were re-purposed for Google+, to capitalize on their SEO value.

This re-prioritization of resources focused the creation of original content to the top channels, conserving resources and maximizing impact.

Marketing Audit Revealed Excellent Sources of Engaging Content

Our initial marketing audit revealed that Lazarex has a large collection of wonderful and emotional stories about their clients. We leveraged this content across social media to inspire and connect with readers.

Facebook post performance for Lazarex Cancer Foundation

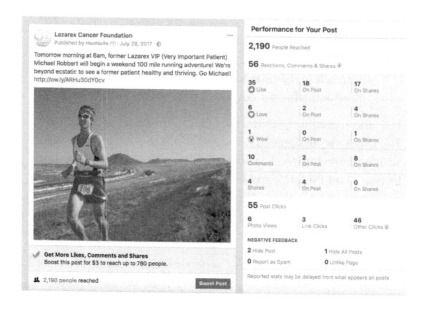

Michael was a former Lazarex Very Important Patient (VIP). He received support from Lazarex to participate in a clinical trial that enabled him to have surgery to remove the cancer from his body and ultimately saved his life.

Now he's back to his love of ultra-marathoning (races of 100 miles or more) and raising money for Lazarex as part of his efforts. Not surprisingly, people love this kind of content. It's inspiring, it's hopeful, it gives anyone touched by cancer (and who doesn't know someone who has been touched by cancer?) hope that there is life after cancer, even after a Stage IV diagnosis in Michael's case.

Ensuring Visual Consistency Across the Brand

In addition to examining the quality of content, we looked at the state of the visual brand assets on displayed on social media. Our finding showed that, although many of the images were beautiful and compelling, there was a wide variety of styles and little consistency between the social pages and the Lazarex brand and website. Inconsistencies in brand image and messaging can lead to viewer confusion and unwanted noise. Here are the Facebook, Twitter, LinkedIn and YouTube visuals before the redesign:

Visuals before the social media visual overhaul

Facebook

Twitter

LinkedIn

YouTube

To combat user confusion and brand inconsistencies, we redesigned the visuals for each page. We designed a strong visual that represents the diversity of the patients Lazarex supports, and focused on presenting a consistent visual brand. Moving between the various social sites and the Lazarex homepage now feels visually and brand consistent, and the primary brand message is reinforced in every channel's masthead image. This leads to a smoother and less confusing user experience.

These are the Facebook, Twitter, LinkedIn and YouTube visuals after the redesign.

Visuals after the social media visual overhaul

Facebook

Twitter

LinkedIn

YouTube

Editorial Calendar Is Crucial to Strategic Social Media Planning

To ensure that all major topics were included in each week's posts, we developed an extensive editorial calendar broken down into the following sections:

1. **Weekly Content Calendar**

   The first step was to list general topics that might be useful, interesting or inspiring that would guide our content development. We made a loose weekly calendar and had specific types of content on certain days, ensuring that important topics were covered every week. This also gave us the flexibility to make adjustments if a time-sensitive news item presented itself. For example, each Wednesday a Lazarex patient story was scheduled which was followed on Fridays with an "in case you missed it" post (hash tagged #ICYMI on Twitter).

2. **Cancer Awareness Dates**

   A focus of the Lazarex mission is to increase awareness of cancer, as cancer caught early is much less likely to be fatal. To support this message, we developed a calendar including a full annual list of cancer awareness days, weeks and months to ensure that Lazarex always had relevant and useful content scheduled for those dates.

3. **Fundraisers and Community Events**

   Lazarex is involved with a number of events throughout the year including many fundraisers and community events. We included these events on the calendar to ensure maximum exposure and promotion.

4. **Cancer Research News**

   We created a list of verified and qualitative news sources that were used to search for shareable content on cancer research that would be helpful for both the general audience and for the pharma industry, which is a key supporter segment.

5. **Hashtag Research**

   We researched which hashtags were most popular in the areas of cancer and cancer research to ensure strategic hashtag use to the proper audience.

6. **Key Influencers**

   We created a list of the reporters, industry leaders, thought leaders and key influencers in health reporting, cancer research, and clinical trial access. We then sought them out and connected with them using Twitter, resulting in relationships with valuable parties.

Once we had completed all our prep work, we set the editorial calendar into motion by filling out the posts for two weeks at a time, leaving room to add in time-sensitive news as it occurred. We tracked the Lazarex website statistics using Google Analytics over time to see how the redesigned social media program was influencing web traffic.

We were excited to see a significant increase in web traffic fairly quickly. Additionally, we saw that visitors routed from social media tended to stay on the site longer, had a lower bounce rate and interacted with more pages. Not only was the social media program driving more people to the website, they were more engaged visitors who are more likely to get involved and donate.

In addition to Google Analytics, we tracked metrics of reach (impressions, followers) and of engagement (e.g., likes, shares, retweets, comments) using our social media management program (Hootsuite) and the native analytics tools from the social channels. We found that human interest and patient stories did very well, as did posts that linked Lazarex with big names such as Joe Biden (Lazarex is part of Joe Biden's Moonshot program), and local news stories that feature the organization.

After a few months of implementing the new social media strategy, Lazarex hit a 12-month high in engagement on LinkedIn in July 2017.

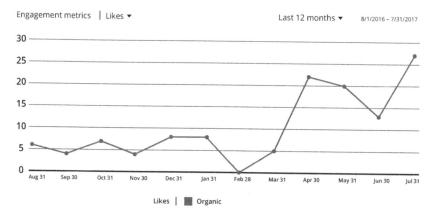

Engagement metrics | Likes ▾   Last 12 months ▾   8/1/2016 – 7/31/2017

Likes | ■ Organic

Knowing these metrics, we refined our editorial calendar accordingly. We focused on posting more content similar to the posts that performed well and posted at times that the analysis showed people were most likely to be online. We found that visitors tended to interact with the site more during business hours than in the evenings or weekends. This surprised us since we did not consider this typical business content. I am always happy to have good data prove me wrong.

By planning the content strategically, then measuring and refining according to the specific feedback from this audience, we combined known best practices in social media marketing with specific audience preferences to drive triple-digit performance for this organization. This strategy can be applied to nearly any business and help to drive their social media program to great success.

Question: Do You Have Resources to Maintain the Channels?

The final question to consider is whether you have the right resources to take care of this critical component of your launch and your ongoing engagement with customers and your community.

Although it does not cost anything to post to social media channels, you will want to either dedicate part or all of a headcount to developing sound social media strategies for your company, and then to managing those channels on an ongoing basis. Several of the startups I've advised at the Microsoft Accelerator get most of their leads from Twitter, for example. Given Twitter's lack of dominance in social media, it seems an unlikely place for leads. However, these startups get this much value from Twitter because they spend most of their social media resources on that channel.

In conclusion, you will get out of social media more than what you put into it if you dedicate someone (internally or externally) to your social media program. If you choose the right channels for your company, and craft a sound social media strategy to create valuable, consistent and engaging content, social media will become one of the best elements in your launch and ongoing success.

Social Strategy Rating Instructions

Please answer the following questions, giving up to two points for each of the five questions below.

Here's a guide on how to rate your answer:

0	1	2
We are seriously lacking	We're ok here, could be better	Got this one nailed

Do you have:

a. The appropriate social media channels set up?	/2
b. A strategy for filling the channels with ongoing content?	/2
c. A strategy for engaging with your target audiences on those channels?	/2
d. Resources to maintain the channels?	/2
e. Qualitative rating	/2

Total: ____ out of 10

Use the qualitative rating to increase or decrease your score to get what seems "right" on a scale of one to ten. This is a chance to soften your ratings if your score for this element seems too low.

This will give you a rating for this element. Transfer this score to the Launch Elements table on page 158.

Once you have scored all 10 elements in this book, add up the individual scores to get your Launch Readiness Score. These questions are also repeated in the final chapter for your convenience, so you have them all in one place there.

9.

Analyzing the Team

Once you have a fully functional product or service definition, and the beginnings of a go-to-market plan for your product, service or company, it's time to start evaluating your team. Do you have the right team members? In the right roles? Are you ready to face the world at, and beyond, launch?

As a company grows, people who were once perfect for certain roles may no longer be perfect for their now expanded roles. I've known founders, for example, who hated it when the company required communications beyond "gathering everyone around the conference table." Clearly that only works when you are 10 or fewer employees. The good part is these founders knew that was their preference and strength. They also knew when it was time to get professional CEOs in to take their companies to the next level of growth.

Know your preferences and strengths as a founder and plan accordingly. And know the preferences and strengths of your management team and act accordingly. People and roles who once fit together nicely may need to be reevaluated in the ramp-up period to the launch. This is the time to make any changes necessary, not right after launch when all eyes are on your company.

Do You Have the Right People in the Right Roles, at the Right Time?

Beyond your role as founder, it's important to have the right team members in the right roles at the right times. For example, one of our clients, a Kleiner Perkins Caufield & Byers startup, hired us to handle all the launch and marketing activities. That made sense, given their position at the time.

As the company grew, the company took on a Chief Marketing Officer (CMO) and then an extended internal marketing team plus us to handle the volume of activity and growth. That was the smart way to manage the growth. I see too many firms rush out and hire a CMO too early who then hires a team of people, creating a fixed cost at a point when growth can be volatile. Grow your team cautiously.

It's also important to have the right roles on your team. Several years ago, we did a Launch Readiness Assessment based on the principles in this book for a key product for a major tech company. They came to us concerned that the revenue from a new product was not doing as well as they had expected.

It was clear from our work during the Assessment that there was little revenue in the current "maker" market, which was a major focus of their marketing activities. Our research showed that the startup market, however, had excellent near-term revenue opportunity. One of their geographical offices, in fact, had been quite successful revenue-wise working with startups locally. We worked with that office to create a translatable model of how to work with the startup market across their other geographies.

Despite the new information and their own successful internal startup go-to-market model, they continued with their previous strategy, focusing on the maker market. In fact, they fully dedicated headcount for the maker market but did not dedicate anyone to the startup market. The product ultimately was discontinued.

Are You Prepared to Speak as a Unified Team to the Outside World?

When evaluating your current team (and yourself), consider whether you are prepared to speak to the outside world as a unified team. When you launch to the world, there will be influencers such as journalists, analysts (for some industries such as tech), potential new investors and, of course, customers who will want to speak with someone and have questions. How will you handle those questions and audiences?

Often in the period leading up to launch, the organization has been heavily engineering and product focused, spending countless hours on developing and refining the product. This is good and appropriate as you want to have a solid, stable, saleable product (see Chapter 1).

As you approach launch, however, the focus needs to turn more outward to ensure that the company is prepared and unified for the outside world's questions. The launch marks the beginning of clear storytelling time about the company.

Here are some of the questions you should ask yourself as you prepare the team for launch and the storytelling phase:

- Do you share a common vision of where the company is headed?
- Can you articulate the reason why people should buy from your company (your value proposition)?
- Do you have a designated spokesperson(s) for media inquiries?
- If analysts are important in your industry, how will you handle analyst briefings?
- How will you handle customer questions and ongoing service for them?

Defining a Common Vision Together with Your Key Players

It's easy for everyone to be running in 10 directions in a startup and lose track of the common vision that unites you. A classic example of this was several years ago during a Brand DNA workshop, which is our proprietary method for extracting and defining the strategic messaging and positioning for a company (see Chapter 2).

I asked the team of this startup about the company vision during the workshop. I got seven different answers. The CEO looked at me and said: "I get it. I have work to do." In fact, he had done nothing wrong. The members of the leadership team in the room had a different vision because they had been so heads down trying to make each of their functions work and work well.

The time had come, however, for us to knit together those disparate views into a common vision. This is part of what the Brand DNA process does — it draws out both the gaps and the common areas and allows us to co-create with the team a common vision to bring the company forward.

The time before launch is the ideal time to galvanize the team around a common vision. It's also the time to define who you are in the world, what you stand for, and why people should buy from you. This sometimes-messy work will define the story that you tell journalists, analysts, new investors and customers.

Your Extended Team: Working with Outside Agencies

Speaking of defining a common vision, setting up extended teams with your agency partners is a critical part of launch. I've seen this done well and done badly. One startup we worked with years ago got to the end of the launch (which was wildly successful), and received a bill from their

PR agency that was almost twice the original quote. This team had gone well beyond the original scope and delivered a fantastic outcome, but the situation was difficult for both the client and the agency.

When working with outside partners such as agencies, there are several things you can do as a client to make the relationship successful. And a successful relationship benefits all parties.

First, be clear about your scope. If you are not sure what the scope is, be willing to pay by the hour, and agree on a "not-to-exceed" (NTE) amount. That could be monthly or a total NTE amount. Make sure you are clear about when you want the budget reviewed. At 50%? At 80%?

Having a budget cap in place would have helped both the client and the PR agency in the story above. Also, be aware that a huge part of the budget can be spent in the last few weeks before a launch, just due to the frenzy that often occurs then. So if you are at 80% and still have three weeks to go before launch, I can guarantee you will be over budget. Sometimes as much as 50% of the budget can be spent in terms of time in the two weeks before launch.

The second thing to put in place when working with outside partners is a regular update cadence. They are not sitting with you every day, so how will you keep them apprised of changes? We like to have at least weekly status meetings with our active clients, which can be one to two hours each week, depending on how much and how fast things are changing. Be as open as possible. The more your agency partners know, the more they can be thinking and strategizing on your behalf.

The third thing to commit to when working with outside partners is to respect their time by making sure you get them the materials and assets they need to help them help you. If you don't provide them key assets, documents or information, you are preventing them from starting or doing their job. Give them what they need to have your back every day. Don't give them an asset the day before the project is due and expect them to turn it around in your timeline. Again, help them help you.

The final thing to think about when working with outside partners is to pay them on time. Or early. This may seem obvious but, when you delay payment, someone needs to take time away from working on your deliverables to check on the payment. You want your outside team fully focused on delivering for you. Late or missing payments make everyone on the team jumpy.

For context, a recent study by Fundbox, a factoring company for small business, found that 64% of small and medium-sized (SMBs) business get paid late and that the total amount in unpaid invoices across all U.S. SMBs is approximately $825 billion. Even more interesting, if all these businesses were paid on time (and agencies are generally SMBs), Fundbox estimates that these SMBs would be able to hire an additional 2.1 million employees, which would reduce unemployment in the U.S. by 27%. By paying your outside teams on time, you will keep them on task by not distracting key players to chase late payments, and you will be doing your part to help the U.S. economy (or whatever economy you are in as these numbers I imagine to be representative of other economies as well).

Get Thee to Media Training!

Once the positioning framework is complete and the messaging defined (either via our Brand DNA Method or some other way), it's time to get media training. If you've not had it before, it's essential that you make it happen now. Journalists are exceedingly short on time — even more so than founders — and it's critical that you learn how to speak to them well. This is important for two major reasons: so that you don't screw up and say something stupid and, more importantly, so that you give journalists the message you want printed or recorded. There is a right and a wrong way to work with the press.

Even if you've had basic media training before, now is a good time to review and train specifically on how to answer questions about your company and the value it delivers (your new messaging). Good media training will cover the most commonly asked questions and techniques on handling hostile questions. Those are more and more rare as journalists are more and more pressed for time, but it's far better to be prepared for that possibility than surprised by it.

I once had a situation personally with an influential Bay Area journalist and his camera crew who were coming to do a feel-good story about the nonprofit where I was a board member. He had planned to interview the executive director that morning, naturally.

Just the night before, however, the Board had been notified that the executive director was resigning, with little notice, and would not be present for the interview. The reporter was displeased that she was not there, and he made that displeasure perfectly clear. I managed to calm him down and we did make the piece into a great story about the organization. I was truly thankful for my years of media experience and training executives on how to handle hostile questions.

Although sometimes media interviews are planned so you can adequately prepare for them, it's not uncommon, especially in the startup world, for media calls to come out of the blue. For this reason, it's best to get this media training well before launch.

That same startup I mentioned earlier received a call from the White House asking the CEO to attend a press conference with the President. Tomorrow. He was in the airport when he received the call, heading out on vacation with his family. He diverted his travel plans to the White House but clearly hadn't had time to prepare fully for such a huge piece of exposure. Fortunately, the messaging had been completed and he'd been media trained a few weeks before so he was ready. The exposure was extremely helpful for this young startup, which was ultimately sold for 10 times its initial investment.

Identifying Your Spokespeople for Launch

A key part of your launch strategy is determining your spokesperson or spokespeople for the launch. That will also define who needs media training since every spokesperson will need media training. The typical suspects for good spokespeople are the CEO, Chief Marketing Officer (CMO), Chief Technical Officer (CTO) or Chief Scientific Officer/Chief Medical Officer (CSO/CMO), depending on your company type.

The CEO and Chief Marketing Officer will be the most commonly used spokespeople for media inquiries. The CTO or CSO/Chief Medical Officer will sometimes be called upon for media inquiries, but will most commonly participate in analyst briefings to help explain the technology or science and answer specific questions.

The rest of your staff, and especially your engineers, should be counseled to direct all media and analyst inquiries to your Chief Marketing Officer so s/he can determine how to proceed. A quick note on social media: the time before launch is also an excellent time to prepare company guidelines on how employees should use social media. See Chapter 8 for details on how to do this.

Engaging with Analysts for Launch

If you are in tech, an analyst strategy should be a key part of your overall launch strategy. Early on, you will want to identify the major analysts covering your space (e.g., Gartner, IDC, Forrester Research). Aside from the usual technology analyst firms, there may be some excellent smaller firms with a laser focus on just that space. CCS Insight, for example, does excellent work in the wearables sector.

So how do you work with analysts? Aside from reading their reports about your market (which you probably used when preparing your pitch deck to define the market), you should engage them early in the launch process.

While I was at PeopleSoft (now Oracle), one analyst shared an analogy that has stuck with me over the years. He said to me, "we like to be involved when you are formulating the recipe, not after you've baked the cake and are icing it." This analogy has served me well in thinking about when to involve analysts in any launch strategy.

When you are working on broad product definitions it is too early to involve analysts, and the month before launch is too late. A good middle ground is when you have the product mostly defined and are in the refinement and building stage. That's when they can give you critical and important feedback about what they are hearing that their customers want. This allows you to leverage their expertise into the product refinements and helps to ensure better market uptake at launch.

You will likely want to arrange for some early pre-briefings under non-disclosure agreements (NDAs) to get their initial feedback early on, and then schedule full briefings the month or so before launch. This way, you get their input early enough to bake it into your cake, and give them enough warning before launch so they are not surprised by your launch announcement and any changes you've made.

For both the pre-briefings and full briefings, you will want to bring in your CTO/CSO/Chief Medical Officer so they can talk in specific detail about the product. Ideally the CEO or Chief Marketing Officer should also participate since the Chief Marketing Officer will likely be the one carrying that relationship with the analyst over time.

I have found that engaging with analysts at this critical time pays off in spades when you do launch the product. If they feel they have had a hand in bringing your product to market and developing a solution they know is what the market needs now, they tend to add lovely icing to your launch cake.

Remember Your Customers — and Those Who Care for Them

It's also important you prep your customer service representatives (CSRs) team. While they are not spokespeople per se, they will be interacting with your customers either on the phone or via email.

Be sure to have a plan for how you will handle the inevitable customer inquiries, either about how to use or set up your product, or how to handle complaints or issues with it. The CSRs should be trained in the company messaging (see Chapter 2) and also be set up for success. They need to be empowered to resolve any issues promptly.

For example, I'm a huge fan of Instacart, an online grocery delivery service that enables me to keep writing while I order groceries in about five minutes to arrive at my doorstep a few hours later. I recently ordered two pounds of potatoes and received two individual potatoes. Clearly that wasn't going to work for the recipe my husband was planning. Plus those two individual potatoes cost $4.98!

I fired off an email to Instacart, via their app, explaining the situation. Within minutes two pounds of potatoes were on their way to our house. It was easy, quick and hassle-free. How will you handle customer inquiries 24/7?

In summary, ensuring you have the right team in place for launch is a key element in its success or failure. Once you are confident that you have the right people in the right roles, the next step is to ensure they are fully prepared for launch with message training, media training, and customer-service training. The launch period is a time of significant change for a young company or division. Make sure your people are prepared for what is about to occur as you turn your focus as a company to a much more outward-facing position.

Team Rating Instructions

Please answer the following questions, giving up to two points for each of the first three questions and up to four for the final, qualitative question.

Here's a guide on how to rate your answer:

0	1	2
We are seriously lacking	We're ok here, could be better	Got this one nailed

Do you have:

a. The right team members?	/2
b. In the right roles?	/2
c. A team prepared to speak as a unified front to the outside world (e.g., press, analysts, investors)?	/2
d. Qualitative rating (use up to four points for this answer)	/4

Total: ____ out of 10

Here is a guide for the qualitative evaluation:

0	1	2	3	4
Our team is really a weak point	We have the bones of a team	We have mostly who we need, a few gaps and some in the wrong roles	We have all the key players we need but the team isn't cohesive yet	Got this one nailed

Use the qualitative rating to increase or decrease your score to get what seems "right" on a scale of one to ten. This is a chance to soften your ratings if your score for this element seems too low.

This will give you a rating for this element. Transfer this score to the Launch Elements table on page 158.

Once you have scored all 10 elements in this book, add up the individual scores to get your Launch Readiness Score. These questions are also repeated in the final chapter for your convenience, so you have them all in one place there.

10.

Finding the Funding

It's an old adage for a reason: You have to spend money to make money. You spend money marketing because you want to increase revenue. There are three basic steps to increasing revenue:

1. Get your solution in front of more people (awareness campaigns)

2. Have more leads (or higher quality leads) coming in for sales to close (lead generation campaigns)

3. Increase your conversion rate (conversion campaigns)

Although we have found that launches can have a mixture of these three objectives, the focus is primarily on increasing awareness of the new product, service or company. Lead generation and conversion tend to be more typical in the post-launch phase.

Do You Have an Appropriate Budget Set Aside to Fund a Successful and Profitable Launch?

In order to increase awareness, lead generation and conversion, you will need to have enough budget to adequately fund the launch. Clients often ask me for ballpark marketing budget numbers. This is clearly dependent on the type of company. Service company marketing budgets are lower than product companies, for example, and B2B companies tend to have smaller budgets than the vast B2C budgets of Proctor & Gamble, for example. That said, there are some good guidelines to consider.

Traditional guidelines have been that about 10% of revenue should be spent on marketing for the average B2B company. Research from Gartner, a technology analyst firm, indicates that on average companies are investing 18% of revenue on marketing. As of August 2017, the twice yearly CMO Survey found that, overall, 6.9% of revenue is being spent on marketing. (That survey is sponsored by the Fuqua School of Business at Duke University, Deloitte LLP, and the American Marketing Association.)

These numbers vary across industries with education at the high end at 18.5% of company revenues set aside for marketing, and energy companies at the lowest end with only 2.2% of company revenues set aside for marketing.

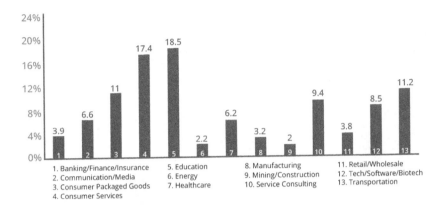

1. Banking/Finance/Insurance   5. Education   8. Manufacturing   11. Retail/Wholesale
2. Communication/Media   6. Energy   9. Mining/Construction   12. Tech/Software/Biotech
3. Consumer Packaged Goods   7. Healthcare   10. Service Consulting   13. Transportation
4. Consumer Services

Source: Highlights and Insights report: https://cmosurvey.org/results/august-2017/

When looking at marketing budgets as a percentage of overall company budgets, the numbers increase. The average is 11.4% set aside for marketing budgets as compared with overall company budgets.

CMOs participating in the August 2017 CMO Report survey reported an actual increase of 6.7% in marketing budgets over the previous 12 months and expected an increase of 8.9% in marketing budgets over the following 12 months. This is good news compared to the February 2009 survey results, when CMOs were expecting a 0.5% budget increase. This increase bodes well for overall economic health.

How Do Market Leaders Allocate Their Marketing Budgets?

Compared to the formal reports like the CMO Report, the research looks a bit different if you look at what successful companies spend on marketing. Turns out that, for successful companies, there are two distinct groupings in the distribution that correlates with the size and age of the company.

Young or high-growth companies, such as Salesforce, Twitter, Marketo and Constant Contact, are spending between 20 to 50%+ on sales and marketing, and seeing anywhere from 15 to 111% increase in revenue. Now that is a great return on a marketing investment!

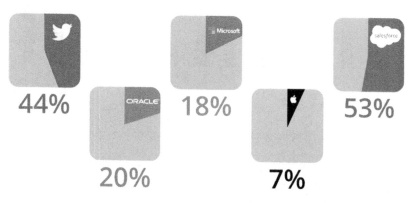

Source: Vital Design

This means that younger companies looking to establish awareness of their brands (i.e., startups) should plan to spend 20 to 50%+ of their budget on marketing. I realize that seems like a lot of money, but chasing a viral video or Kickstarter campaign is a long shot. Stick with the basics and execute, execute, execute.

Also interesting to note in this research was that larger, more mature companies such as Intel, Microsoft and Apple tended to spend a smaller percentage of their budget on sales and marketing. Of course, their revenue is substantial so 7% of Apple's revenue is nearly $12 billion.

This shift to a lower percentage of budget for mature companies makes sense in terms of the percentage of revenue. For them, that's still a lot of money with which to make noise in the market. Also, established companies don't have to spend as much on awareness campaigns since their brand recognition is extremely high.

And larger, more established companies need to be more focused on lead generation and conversion metrics. In this type of situation, it tends to be more about gaining percentages of market share in terms of overall marketing wins, and the budget needs to be allocated accordingly.

Is the Budget Sufficient?

Based on the discussion above, and your type of company, do you have what you need? Use either the "as a percentage of revenue" or "as a percentage of overall budgets" guideline to see where you stand. As a startup, you will need to figure out how to get that budget to fund the launch for your company or product.

Without an adequate budget, you will likely be relegated to the 92% failure rate of startups. Great products do NOT sell themselves. Look at the budgets for consumer packaged goods. Companies spend marketing money, serious money, on toilet paper. So it's important not to bootstrap too tightly.

In larger companies, the budgeting process tends to be more structured but it's always possible to find more budget — if you can present a strong argument about how the money will be used and the type of revenue your plan will deliver. The current CMO Survey will be a useful benchmarking tool to set expectations about what other organizations like yours are doing in the marketplace.

Even large companies can be at risk of a launch failure without a proper marketing budget. This is particularly true if the product is in a new market, which is outside the typical dimensions of the brand. At that point, you are essentially a startup within a larger organization. It's often a little easier to have a zero-based budget in a larger company, particularly if your new division is seen as the future direction of the company. The big challenge for large company skunkworks projects is making sure your work is "visible," but that's a topic for a whole other book.

Is that Budget Readily Available in Time for Your Planned Launch?

Once you've crunched your numbers and know you have sufficient budget, make sure that money is actually in your account if you are a startup, and not "pending" from your venture capital (VC) firm. You can't market with dollars you don't have.

Also confirm that you will have the money in your account with enough lead time to properly prepare for your launch. That means you need that funding three to six months before launch.

I know that having the money in hand seems obvious but I cannot tell you how many times I've talked with startups who were madly spending marketing budget they didn't have yet, or making marketing plans with dollars they didn't yet have. So clearly, this point is not obvious to a lot of people.

In summary, to prepare properly for launch, you will need sufficient budget to drive awareness of your new product, service or company. Use the benchmarks above to figure out some guideline for your particular situation. Then make sure that budget is readily available within the timeline you have set for launch and press forward, knowing you have all the elements you need for a successful launch.

Funding Rating Instructions

Please answer the following questions, giving up to two points for each of the first three questions and up to four for the final, qualitative question.

Here's a guide on how to rate your answer:

0	1	2
We are seriously lacking	We're ok here, could be better	Got this one nailed

Do you have an appropriate budget that:

a. Can fund the additional activities of a successful and profitable launch?	/2
b. Is readily available?	/2
c. Is sufficient?	/2
d. Qualitative rating (use up to four points for this answer)	/4

Total: __ out of 10

Here is a guide for the qualitative evaluation:

0	1	2	3	4
Our lack of funding is a weak point	We have some funding but it's in a variety of locations/sources	We have mostly what we need, but something is lacking (timing, etc.)	We have funding but aren't sure how to allocate it	Got this one nailed

Use the qualitative rating to increase or decrease your score to get what seems "right" on a scale of one to ten. This is a chance to soften your ratings if your score for this element seems too low.

This will give you a rating for this element. Transfer this score to the Launch Elements table on page 158.

Once you have scored all 10 elements in this book, add up the individual scores to get your Launch Readiness Score. These questions are also repeated in the final chapter for your convenience, so you have them all in one place there.

Summing It All Up

Your Launch Action Plan

The time has come to bring together all the elements we have reviewed in the previous chapters. Here are the questions for each element. You can transfer your scores from the individual chapters, or rate your readiness here. Later in this chapter, you can add up your individual scores to get your overall Launch Readiness Score.

Element 1: Offering Rating Instructions

Please answer the following questions, giving up to two points for each of the five questions below.

Here's a guide on how to rate your answer:

0	1	2
We are seriously lacking	We're ok here, could be better	Got this one nailed

Is the product/service/offering:

a. Fully functional?	/2
b. Easy for your target market to use?	/2
c. Covered by appropriate legal protections and/or complies with regulatory guidelines?	/2
d. Covered by appropriate IP filings?	/2
e. Qualitative rating	/2

Total: ___ out of 10

Use the qualitative rating to increase or decrease your score to get what seems "right" on a scale of one to ten. This is a chance to soften your ratings if your score for this element seems too low.

This will give you a rating for this element. Transfer this score to the Launch Elements table at the end of this section.

Element 2: Positioning Rating Instructions

Please answer the following questions, giving up to two points for each of the first three questions and up to four for the final, qualitative question.

Here's a guide on how to rate your answer:

0	1	2
We are seriously lacking	We're ok here, could be better	Got this one nailed

Do you have:

a. Clearly defined positioning?	/2
b. With a differentiated message?	/2
c. A message that resonates with your target audience?	/2
d. Qualitative rating	/4

Total: ____ out of 10

Here is a guide for the qualitative evaluation:

0	1	2	3	4
We are seriously lacking	It's not terrible	We're ok here, could be better	We are getting there, still missing something	Got this one nailed

Use the qualitative rating to increase or decrease your score to get what seems "right" on a scale of one to ten. This is a chance to soften your ratings if your score for this element seems too low.

This will give you a rating for this element. Transfer this score to the Launch Elements table at the end of this section.

Element 3: Naming Rating Instructions

Please answer the following questions, giving up to two points for each of the five questions below.

Here's a guide on how to rate your answer:

0	1	2
We are seriously lacking	We're ok here, could be better	Got this one nailed

Does your offering (product/service/company) have a name that:

a.	Is memorable? Easy to say and spell?	/2
b.	Has positive connotations?	/2
c.	Has been tested in the major languages/markets in which you plan to sell?	/2
d.	Is available in your category (trademark protection) and as a good URL?	/2
e.	Qualitative rating	/2

Total: ____ out of 10

Use the qualitative rating to increase or decrease your score to get what seems "right" on a scale of one to ten. This is a chance to soften your ratings if your score for this element seems too low.

This will give you a rating for this element. Transfer this score to the Launch Elements table at the end of this section.

Element 4: Logo Rating Instructions

Please answer the following questions, giving up to two points for each of the five questions below.

Here's a guide on how to rate your answer:

0	1	2
We are seriously lacking	We're ok here, could be better	Got this one nailed

Is your logo:

a. Clean?	/2
b. Simple (with no more than three elements)?	/2
c. Useable at all sizes (very small to billboard size)?	/2
d. Reflective of your brand promise?	/2
e. Qualitative rating	/2

Total: ____ out of 10

Use the qualitative rating to increase or decrease your score to get what seems "right" on a scale of one to ten. This is a chance to soften your ratings if your score for this element seems too low.

This will give you a rating for this element. Transfer this score to the Launch Elements table at the end of this section.

Element 5: Website Rating Instructions

Please answer the following questions, giving up to two points for each of the five questions below.

Here's a guide on how to rate your answer:

0	1	2
We are seriously lacking	We're ok here, could be better	Got this one nailed

For your online presence:

a. Do you have a website developed for the initiative?	/2
b. Do you own the actual name as a URL?	/2
c. Have you developed a domain strategy?	/2
d. Does your website tell your brand story well?	/2
e. Qualitative rating	/2

Total: ____ out of 10

Use the qualitative rating to increase or decrease your score to get what seems "right" on a scale of one to ten. This is a chance to soften your ratings if your score for this element seems too low.

This will give you a rating for this element. Transfer this score to the Launch Elements table at the end of this section.

Note: If you have more than one website for your initiative, average the score across the properties to get a sum out of 10.

Element 6: Sales Strategy Rating Instructions

Please answer the following questions, giving up to two points for each of the five questions below.

Here's a guide on how to rate your answer:

0	1	2
We are seriously lacking	We're ok here, could be better	Got this one nailed

Do you have:

a. A defined sales strategy?	/2
b. A process for handling incoming leads?	/2
c. Consistent sales materials?	/2
d. Sales tools and training?	/2
e. Qualitative rating	/2

Total: ____ out of 10

Use the qualitative rating to increase or decrease your score to get what seems "right" on a scale of one to ten. This is a chance to soften your ratings if your score for this element seems too low.

This will give you a rating for this element. Transfer this score to the Launch Elements table at the end of this section.

Element 7: Content Strategy Rating Instructions

Please answer the following questions, giving up to two points for each of the five questions below.

Here's a guide on how to rate your answer:

0	1	2
We are seriously lacking	We're ok here, could be better	Got this one nailed

Do you have:

a. A mix of content types?	/2
b. Content that can be delivered at various points in the sales cycle?	/2
c. Engaging content that draws people to your brand?	/2
d. A strategy for delivering content appropriately?	/2
e. Qualitative rating	/2

Total: ____ out of 10

Use the qualitative rating to increase or decrease your score to get what seems "right" on a scale of one to ten. This is a chance to soften your ratings if your score for this element seems too low.

This will give you a rating for this element. Transfer this score to the Launch Elements table at the end of this section.

Element 8: Social Strategy Rating Instructions

Please answer the following questions, giving up to two points for each of the five questions below.

Here's a guide on how to rate your answer:

0	1	2
We are seriously lacking	We're ok here, could be better	Got this one nailed

Do you have:

a.	The appropriate social media channels set up?	/2
b.	A strategy for filling the channels with ongoing content?	/2
c.	A strategy for engaging with your target audiences on those channels?	/2
d.	Resources to maintain the channels?	/2
e.	Qualitative rating	/2

Total: ____ out of 10

Use the qualitative rating to increase or decrease your score to get what seems "right" on a scale of one to ten. This is a chance to soften your ratings if your score for this element seems too low.

This will give you a rating for this element. Transfer this score to the Launch Elements table at the end of this section.

Element 9: Team Rating Instructions

Please answer the following questions, giving up to two points for each of the first three questions and up to four for the final, qualitative question.

Here's a guide on how to rate your answer:

0	1	2
We are seriously lacking	We're ok here, could be better	Got this one nailed

Do you have:

a.	The right team members?	/2
b.	In the right roles?	/2
c.	A team prepared to speak as a unified front to the outside world (e.g., press, analysts, investors)?	/2
d.	Qualitative rating	/4

Total: ___ out of 10

Here is a guide for the qualitative evaluation:

0	1	2	3	4
Our team is really a weak point	We have the bones of a team	We have mostly who we need, a few gaps and some in the wrong roles	We have all the key players we need but the team isn't cohesive yet	Got this one nailed

Use the qualitative rating to increase or decrease your score to get what seems "right" on a scale of one to ten. This is a chance to soften your ratings if your score for this element seems too low.

This will give you a rating for this element. Transfer this score to the Launch Elements table at the end of this section.

Element 10: Funding Rating Instructions

Please answer the following questions, giving up to two points for each of the first three questions and up to four for the final, qualitative question.

Here's a guide on how to rate your answer:

0	1	2
We are seriously lacking	We're ok here, could be better	Got this one nailed

Do you have an appropriate budget set that:

a.	Can fund the additional activities of a successful and profitable launch?	/2
b.	Is readily available?	/2
c.	Is sufficient?	/2
d.	Qualitative rating (use up to four points for this answer)	/4

Total: ____ out of 10

Here is a guide for the qualitative evaluation:

0	1	2	3	4
Our lack of funding is a weak point	We have some funding but it's in a variety of locations/ sources	We have mostly what we need, but something is lacking (timing, etc.)	We have funding but aren't sure how to allocate it	Got this one nailed

Use the qualitative rating to increase or decrease your score to get what seems "right" on a scale of one to ten. This is a chance to soften your ratings if your score for this element seems too low.

This will give you a rating for this element. Transfer this score to the Launch Elements table at the end of this section.

Now you can take all your individual launch element scores and write them in here:

Launch Element	Score
Element 1: Offering	/10
Element 2: Positioning	/10
Element 3: Name	/10
Element 4: Logo	/10
Element 5: Website	/10
Element 6: Sales Strategy	/10
Element 7: Content	/10
Element 8: Social Strategy	/10
Element 9: Team	/10
Element 10: Funding	/10
LAUNCH READINESS SCORE	%

Wondering How Your Score Compares?

Based on responses from the online self-assessment version of the Launch Readiness Assessment and from direct work we've done with clients here in Silicon Valley, most scores range between 50% and close to 80% readiness. The majority are in the 60 to 70% range.

What tends to vary is which elements need the most work. This is where more careful analysis is required. Sometimes it's obvious — pick the lowest three scores and shore those up before launch.

Sometimes figuring out where to focus your time, resources and budget is trickier. For example, if the name is an issue — either because you've discovered it's already taken or it's hard for people to pronounce or hear — you must fix that before you can attend to the logo redesign. If the logo needs to be redesigned, you need to do that before you start the website design since the logo colors will drive the website color palette. The thigh bone is connected to the hip bone at many points in marketing.

Here are some guidelines to help prioritize the elements of your launch, based on your Launch Readiness Score.

- Focus on the weakest areas. Some will be easy to shore up. Others will take more time and work.

- Give yourself adequate time and budget.

- Plan on at least three to six months for a successful launch.

- Expect to see lasting results within six to nine months of the launch.

Also look at what activities will need to be done to shore up those weaker elements. Do you have the skills/expertise/people/time to do those easily? Or do you need to find additional resources? Understanding the difference leads into how the Launch Action Plan is developed from the Launch Readiness Score.

Example of a Launch Action Plan

The Launch Action Plan is your roadmap to a successful launch. It's an actionable list of the tasks and activities needed to ensure you are truly ready to launch and be successful in the marketplace.

In preparing clients for a launch, I try not to overwhelm them with a super-long list of actions right out of the gate. So we generally group the activities into three sets:

1. "Do Now" — These tasks are generally done in the first few weeks of implementation

2. "Do Soon" — These tasks can be done shortly after the "Do Now" tasks are completed, or at least started

3. "Do When You Can" — These tasks can be done as time allows

This is an example of a Launch Action Plan produced following a Launch Readiness Assessment for a ThinkResults client.

Sample Launch Action Plan of key activities

DO NOW

- Color palette definition
- Start consolidating brands
- Start transition to new brand (develop new logo, colors, etc.)
- Develop a strong Facebook and YouTube content strategy to increase engagement
- Ensure all new collateral and event invites are consistent with the brand
- Clarify messages on website via content and navigation changes
- Content update to site to make messages clearer

DO SOON

- Proactive PR with media planning and outreach (depending on expected news cycle)
- Develop email editorial calendar (newsletter and eBlasts)
- Consolidate social media channel visuals
- Execute on Facebook and YouTube strategy
- SEO research and then optimize pages (start with main site)
- Visual upgrades to key pages

DO WHEN YOU CAN

- Various minor web edits
- Merge two Google+ pages

In the above example, several groupings of actions need to be taken to ensure the client is on track for a successful launch. The first grouping is the "Do Now" set of tasks.

These "Do Now" actions tend to be those that will have the biggest impact on the launch success, or are just plain are easy to do. For example, in this case, the proliferation of brands was having a strong negative effect on resources for this client. As part of our Assessment for them, we looked at their overall brand architecture and identified which of the sub-brands made sense to continue with (a small list) and which ones needed to be "unbranded" or to come under the master brand.

This brand consolidation conserved time and money. Also, a more streamlined set of brands with a stronger master brand made it much easier for the public to understand this organization. That's what I call a win-win-win.

Sometimes, the "Do Now" tasks are simpler than this example, but the tasks can impact many downstream items so we need to get them done ASAP. In this case, the original color palette needed to be expanded and properly defined for the graphics people to ensure flexibility and consistency. While this is not a challenging task (although it can be since color is an emotionally charged topic), the decision impacts all other graphics so it was a "Do Now" and almost a "Do First" Action Item.

The "Do Soon" items tend to be those that are dependent on a "Do Now" task or ones that can wait a bit before being initiated. These activities tend to be more complex in nature or may require additional budget than the "Do Now" group.

For example, we wanted to consolidate the colors and imagery on the social media channels to ensure brand consistency, but we first needed to define the new messages, visual direction and color palette for the website home page.

It also didn't make sense to do proactive media outreach until we had completed some of the strategic brand consolidation, and had clear, consistent messaging and visuals on the website and social channels. You do not want to drive a bunch of traffic to your site and channels through PR, email and SEO work until those properties are clean and consistent in terms of messaging and the brand visuals.

The final category is the "Do When You Can" list. These activities, by themselves, do not have a huge impact. However, they are fairly simple to do and can add up in terms of cumulative impact. In this case, we gave the technical web team a list of technical issues that needed to be cleaned up on the website. There were multiple Google+ pages that also needed to be cleaned up, but they weren't a top priority.

It takes a bit of experience to decide what needs to be done and in what order. Use the ranking of those items that scored the lowest in your assessment to guide you. And engage a marketing expert to help you if you get lost.

The Special Case of Relaunching

Relaunching carries some special challenges, in addition to all the guidance presented in this book. Some relaunches are from the ground up and include everything from re-naming to a new logo and through all the elements of launch. Some are more contained (although equally complicated) and are focused more on repositioning. In any of these scenarios, unlike an initial company launch, you will have to "fix the plane as it's flying." You have to keep the business running (and generating revenue) while you are relaunching it for future growth.

Having a separate team that is focused on the relaunch will enable your current marketing team to focus on the day-to-day marketing that is currently driving the revenue in the company. A word of warning: having been through many relaunches, I can say there will be several times when team members will become impatient to get the launch over and done. This impatience will grow once the new creative is done and approved. Give your launch team the time and space they need to fully complete launch preparations. This can be as delicate as a rocket launch. Don't take anyone out in the rush to "make it so."

A Few Final Thoughts on Launching Well

A few final things to think about when planning your launch. As I've mentioned before, leave enough time and money in your plan for launch. Our research and experience shows that three to six months is the ideal launch timeline.

In terms of budget, check out the Funding chapter for specific details. Remember that the launch is also the time to do some "extras" in terms of marketing.

A launch is a unique time for your company, product or service, so it's the time to think about some of those things you might not normally do, such as print advertising, or sponsorship of a key event or two in your market. You may do those things normally (depending on the size of your company) but launch is the time to really double down and be the "platinum" sponsor or do other marketing "splurges." The launch period is usually short so the bigger impact you can make for those two to three days, the better.

And speaking of the launch period, I often get asked if a company should do one big launch event and save everything for that day, or should the launch activities be spread out. This is a delicate question. Doing a "hard" launch (everything or nearly everything is released on a specific date or at a key event) tends to have the most impact in terms of the highest peak of response. It is also the hardest way to launch as you have to "save" everything up for that event or day. These types of launches are most typically done when the launch has been promised to investors or customers by a certain date, or when there is an important conference or event that makes good sense to use as your launch event.

As a result, "hard launches" tend to be used more often by larger, public companies. They require more coordination and are harder and generally more expensive to do.

A "soft" launch is one where the launch elements are released over time. Even soft launches tend to have one or more "launch events" when groups of elements are released. Perhaps the new name, logo and website are launched on a particular go-live date, with some key content marketing, PR and social media supporting those elements. Then, more elements are released later at a key conference, for example. This secondary launch event may have some additional content (e.g., collateral, lead magnets, email) and social media as part of that event. In this way, a series of launch events are part of your overall launch strategy.

In a way, hard launches tend to have a bit of soft-launch, rolling-thunder launch elements as part of them, and soft launches have some hard-launch elements. Again, it can be tricky to decide which makes the most sense for you, and which approach will have the most impact. Generally, my recommendation is to go with a soft launch with a defined major launch event/date followed by several mini-launch events/dates in the following months. That gives you the most flexibility. It also allows you to tailor the mini-launch events to focus on a particular facet of the product or key audience.

Another important consideration in planning your launch is getting buy-in from management. I'd like to give advice about how to do this. Unfortunately, after many years in this business, the main thing I know is that if senior management has not bought into the importance of a good launch, the chances that you will "convince" them are slim. Never take a role in which you are constantly having to prove your worth to the company or fight for appropriate budget.

In terms of evaluating the launch, ideally you have set clear metrics at the beginning of the process. Measuring awareness can be a complex and therefore expensive proposition. At least for our startups, we usually take news coverage as a proxy for increasing awareness. Social media reach and engagement can also be good proxies for awareness, without having to do formal (and often expensive) awareness market research.

Often there are lead expectations around a launch and those kinds of metrics can make it much easier to measure success. The key is to define the metric ahead of time. You can always add new ones later but you will want to know before you start whether awareness or leads are your prime focus for the launch as that will impact your strategy and tactics.

One final note about launches and launch strategy. This is a marathon, not a sprint. Too often, I've seen teams nearly kill themselves getting everything ready for a launch or launch event, and then not have any time, energy or budget left after the big event. This is a mistake. As I mentioned, the best launches tend to have a rolling-thunder cadence. A big boom, followed by a series of smaller booms. Don't spend all your time, energy and money on the big boom. Plan for the thunder to roll. It's much more effective and less exhausting for the launch team.

And remember to celebrate what you have achieved. After the "big" launch event is the perfect time for kudos all around, as well as a debrief on what worked well and what could be better. It will help your team regain energy for the rolling-thunder elements still to come.

Join Our Community

If you'd like to delve deeper, we have a special section on my author website just for readers of *Launching for Revenue*, with additional information, case studies and examples on each of the 10 elements. We just couldn't fit all the information in this book and new examples pop up all the time. We will add to this over time to give you the latest and greatest information in your Launching for Revenue community. On this site, you can also ask questions and get feedback from me. You'll need your Launch Readiness Score (don't worry — we won't share it publicly) as your special passcode to get into the website:

JenniferSLeBlanc.com/Launching-Community

By now you probably get that I believe in systems. I did things the hard way many times and developed this system both to simplify my life and to improve our effectiveness for our clients. This system has been time-tested, and has helped us successfully launch and re-launch companies, products and services. We hope you find the information as valuable as we have.

Good luck on your launch. Please let us know how things are going. We'd love to see you online at the free Launching for Revenue Community. In the meantime, a toast to your successful launch!

Resources and Sources

Resources

Several authors have influenced the thinking in this book. If you have not already read these books, I highly recommend you do so:

Jim Collins, *Good to Great: Why Some Companies Make the Leap … and Others Don't*

Seth Godin, *Purple Cow: Transform Your Business by Being Remarkable; Permission Marketing: Turning Strangers into Friends, and Friends into Customers*

Malcom Gladwell, *The Tipping Point: How Little Things Can Make a Big Difference*

Lisa Goldman and Kate Purmal, *The Moonshot Effect: Disrupting Business As Usual*

Anne H. Janzer, *Subscription Marketing; The Writer's Process; The Workplace Writer's Process*

Guy Kawasaki, *The Art of the Start 2.0: The Time-Tested, Battle-Hardened Guide for Anyone Starting Anything*

Geoffrey A. Moore, *Crossing the Chasm: Marketing and Selling High-tech Products to Mainstream Customers; Escape Velocity: Free Your Company's Future from the Pull of the Past; Living on the Fault Line: Managing for Shareholder Value in the Age of the Internet*

Daniel H. Pink, *To Sell Is Human: The Surprising Truth About Moving Others; When: The Scientific Secrets of Perfect Timing*

Linda J. Popky, *Marketing Above the Noise: Achieving Strategic Advantage with Marketing that Matters*

Al Ries and Jack Trout, *The 22 Immutable Laws of Marketing: Violate Them at Your Own Risk!; Positioning: The Battle for Your Mind*

Eric Ries, *The Lean Startup*

Lewis Schiff, *Business Brilliant: How to Build Wealth, Manage Your Career & Take Risks*

Lisa B. Stambaugh, *Web Diva Wisdom: How to Find, Hire, and Partner with the Right Web Designer for You*

Sources

Introduction

Badal, Sangeeta. (October 23, 2014). *Gallup Business Journal.* Retrieved from http://www.gallup.com/businessjournal/178787/why-new-companies-fail-during-first-five-years.aspx

Castellion, George and Markham, Stephen K. (October 25, 2012). *Journal of Product Innovation & Management.* Retrieved from http://goo.gl/M88dA5

Castellion, George and Markham, Stephen K. (n.d.). *Myths About New Product Failure Rates*. Retrieved December 31, 2017, from http://newproductsuccess.org/white-papers/new-product-failure-rates-2013-jpim-30-pp-976-979/

Marmer, Max; Herrmann, Bjoern Lasse; Dogrultan, Ertan; Berman, Ron. (2012, March). *Startup Genome Report*. Retrieved from https://s3.amazonaws.com/startupcompass-public/StartupGenomeReport1_Why_Startups_Succeed_v2.pdf

Chapter 1: Developing the Offering

Reis, Eric. (2011). *The Lean Startup: How Today's Entrepreneurs Use Continuous Innovation to Create Radically Successful Businesses* (1st ed.). United States of America: Crown Publishing Group

W3 Schools. (n.d.). *Browser Statistics*. Retrieved December 31, 2017, from https://www.w3schools.com/browsers/

Wikipedia. (n.d.). *Minimal Viable Products*. Retrieved July 14, 2017, from https://en.wikipedia.org/wiki/Minimum_viable_product

Chapter 2: Defining the Positioning

Bilton, Nick. (December 9, 2009). *The American Diet: 34 Gigabytes a Day*. Retrieved from https://bits.blogs.nytimes.com/2009/12/09/the-american-diet-34-gigabytes-a-day/?mcubz=0

Godin, Seth. (November 12, 2009). *Purple Cow: Transform Your Business by Being Remarkable*. New York: Portfolio.

Kawasaki, Guy. (March 3, 2015). *Art of the Start 2.0: The Time-Tested, Battle-Hardened Guide for Anyone Starting Anything*. New York: Portfolio.

Mankani, Mahjabeen. (August 31, 2012). *Advertising Analysis – 7UP Time*. Retrieved from https://www.dawn.com/news/746001

Ries, Al and Trout, Jack. (2000). *Positioning: The Battle for Your Mind*. New York: McGraw-Hill Education.

Chapter 3: Choosing a Name (or a New Name)

Accenture. (October 26, 2000). *Andersen Consulting Announces New Name — Accenture — Effective 01.01.01.* Retrieved from https://newsroom.accenture.com/subjects/accenture-corporate/andersen-consulting-announces-new-name-accenture-effective-010101.htm

Bushnaq, Margot. (March 31, 2009). *Another Post-Scandal Corporate Name Change.* Retrieved from https://www.brandbucket.com/blog/another-post-scandal-corporate-name-change

Despres, Tricia. (April 9, 2013). *5 of the Worst Rebranding Disasters.* Retrieved from http://www.ragan.com/Main/Articles/5_of_the_worst_rebranding_disasters_46493.aspx

Harness, Jill. (September 10, 2009). *Companies Renamed to Hide From Bad Reputations.* Retrieved from http://www.neatorama.com/2009/09/10/companies-renamed-to-hide-from-bad-reputations/

Mikkelson, Barbara. (July 26, 2014). *Incubus Shoe.* Retrieved from http://www.snopes.com/business/market/incubus.asp

List of renamed products. (n.d.). In Wikipedia. Retrieved September 24, 2017, from https://en.wikipedia.org/wiki/List_of_renamed_products

Chapter 4: Designing the Logo

Humphrey, Amber. (August 25, 2016). *Less is More: The Power of Negative Space Logos.* Retrieved from https://www.deluxe.com/sbrc/logo/less-is-more-the-power-of-negative-space-logos

Raghav, Saumya. (March 23, 2016). *Starbucks Logo – An Overview of Design, History and Evolution.* Retrieved from https://www.designhill.com/design-blog/starbucks-logo-overview-of-design-history-and-evolution/

Chapter 5: Developing the Website

Chaffey, Dave. (April 11, 2017). *Mobile Share of Online Time Percent 2017 –US, UK, China, Canada, Mexico.* Retrieved from http://www.smartinsights.com/mobile-marketing/mobile-marketing-analytics/mobile-marketing-statistics/attachment/mobile-share-of-online-time-percent-2017/

Culp-Ressler, Tara. (October 23, 2014). *Men's Rights Group Masquerades as Fake Domestic Violence Campaign to Confuse Donors.* Retrieved from https://thinkprogress.org/mens-rights-group-masquerades-as-fake-domestic-violence-campaign-to-confuse-donors-6837c27cc90d#.8e9cxj5zj

Gartner. (n.d.). *The Digital Evolution in B2B Marketing.* Retrieved on February 3, 2017, from https://www.cebglobal.com/marketing-communications/digital-evolution.html/

Haile, Tony. (March 9, 2014). *What You Think You Know About the Web Is All Wrong.* Retrieved from http://time.com/12933/what-you-think-you-know-about-the-web-is-wrong/

Lella, Adam and Lipsman, Andrew. (March 30, 2016). *2016 U.S. Cross-Platform Future in Focus.* Retrieved from http://www.comscore.com/Insights/Presentations-and-Whitepapers/2016/2016-US-Cross-Platform-Future-in-Focus

Miller, Cody Ray. (n.d.). *The 59 Second Rule: 3 Reasons Why Users Leave a Website.* Retrieved from https://blog.crazyegg.com/2013/07/19/why-users-leave-a-website/

Nielsen, Jakob. (September 12, 2011). *How Long Do Users Stay on Web Pages?* Retrieved from https://www.nngroup.com/articles/how-long-do-users-stay-on-web-pages/

Sterling, Greg. (April 3, 2016). *All Digital Growth Now Coming From Mobile Usage — comScore.* Retrieved from http://marketingland.com/digital-growth-now-coming-mobile-usage-comscore-171505

Tribune Content Solutions. (August 21, 2013). *Reasons You Should Stop Using Flash.* Retrieved from http://tribunecontentsolutions.com/blog/2013/08/21/reasons-you-should-stop-using-flash/

Chapter 6: Setting the Sales Strategy

Connick, Wendy. (n.d.). *The Seven Stages of the Sales Cycle.* Retrieved on July 16, 2017, from https://www.nasp.com/article/AE1B7061-3F39/the-seven-stages-of-the-sales-cycle.html

Chapter 7: Crafting the Content Strategy

@smfrogers. (March 10, 2014). *What Fuels a Tweet's Engagement?* Retrieved from https://blog.twitter.com/official/en_us/a/2014/what-fuels-a-tweets-engagement.html

Agrawal, AJ. (December 15, 2016). *17 Marketing Trends to Watch Out for in 2017.* Retrieved from https://www.forbes.com/sites/ajagrawal/2016/12/15/17-marketing-trends-to-watch-out-for-2017/#6dd3e25a28ef

Brenner, Michael. (March 2, 2017). *Content Marketing Trends to Watch Out for in 2017.* Retrieved from https://marketinginsidergroup.com/content-marketing/content-marketing-trends-2017-infographic/

Covey, Stephen R. (2004). *The 7 Habits of Highly Effective People.* New York: Fireside

Learning Styles Online. (n.d.). *Overview of Learning Styles.* Retrieved on July 16, 2017, from https://www.learning-styles-online.com/overview/

Pant, Ritu. (January 16, 2015). *Visual Marketing: A Picture's Worth 60,000 Words.* Retrieved from http://www.business2community.com/digital-marketing/visual-marketing-pictures-worth-60000-words-01126256#THMZgiAhhGHtshd6.97

Pulizzi, Joe. (December 19, 2016). *Five Content Marketing Trends to Watch in 2017*. Retrieved from http://contentmarketinginstitute.com/2016/12/content-marketing-trends-watch/

Sutter, Brian. (December 2, 2016). 8 *Trends that Will Shape Content Marketing in 2017*. Retrieved from https://www.forbes.com/sites/briansutter/2016/12/02/8-trends-that-will-shape-content-marketing-in-2017/4/#7b08959b4fbb

Trafton, Anne. (January 16, 2014). *In the Blink of an Eye*. Retrieved from http://news.mit.edu/2014/in-the-blink-of-an-eye-0116

Chapter 8: Setting the Social Strategy

AdWeek. (April 4, 2016). *Here's How Many People Are on Facebook, Instagram, Twitter and Other Big Social Networks*. Retrieved from http://www.adweek.com/digital/heres-how-many-people-are-on-facebook-instagram-twitter-other-big-social-networks/

Apus, Randy. (October 20, 2014). *Social Media User Statistics & Age Demographics for 2014*. Retrieved from http://jetscram.com/blog/industry-news/social-media-user-statistics-and-age-demographics-2014/

Aslam, Salman. (January 1, 2018). *LinkedIn by the Numbers: Stats, Demographics & Fun Facts*. Retrieved from https://www.omnicoreagency.com/linkedin-statistics/

Bagadiya, Jimit. (January 8, 2018). 171 *Amazing Social Media Statistics You Should Know in 2018*. Retrieved from https://socialpilot.co/blog/151-amazing-social-media-statistics-know-2017/

Bullas, Jeff. (n.d.). *25 LinkedIn Facts and Statistics You Need to Share*. Retrieved January 28, 2018, from http://www.jeffbullas.com/25-linkedin-facts-and-statistics-you-need-to-share/

Choate, Dave. (September 27, 2016). *What Is Google Plus in 2017, and Who's Using It?* Retrieved from https://www.rakacreative.com/blog/social-media/what-is-google-plus-2016/

Fontein, Dara. (November 28, 2016). *The Pinterest Statistics That Matter to Your Business.* Retrieved from https://blog.hootsuite.com/pinterest-statistics-for-business/

Gesenhues, Amy. (May 13, 2015). *YouTube "How To" Video Searches Up 70%, With Over 100 Million Hours Watched in 2015.* Retrieved from https://searchengineland.com/youtube-how-to-searches-up-70-yoy-with-over-100m-hours-of-how-to-videos-watched-in-2015-220773

Griffis, Hailley. (November 10, 2016). *5 Surprising Reasons to Reconsider Google+ (That You Can Act on Today).* Retrieved from https://blog.bufferapp.com/google-plus

Hutchinson, Andrew. (March 21, 2017). *Top Social Network Demographics 2017* [Infographic]. Retrieved from http://www.socialmediatoday.com/social-networks/top-social-network-demographics-2017-infographic

Kallas, Prit. (January 16, 2018). *Top 15 Most Popular Social Networking Sites and Apps* [January 2018]. Retrieved from https://www.dreamgrow.com/top-15-most-popular-social-networking-sites/

Mathison, Rob. (January 24, 2018). *23+ Useful Instagram Statistics for Social Media Marketers.* Retrieved from https://blog.hootsuite.com/instagram-statistics/

MediaKix. (February 7, 2017). *Are Top Influencers Leaving Snapchat for Instagram?* Retrieved from http://mediakix.com/2017/02/top-influencers-leaving-snapchat-for-instagram/

MediaKix. (February 7, 2017). *Is Snapchat Dying? User Growth, App Downloads, Trends.* Retrieved from http://mediakix.com/2017/02/is-snapchat-dying-user-growth-app-downloads-trends/#gs.Go5KHM8

MediaKix. (November 10, 2017). *The Snapchat Statistics Every Marketer Needs to Know.* Retrieved from http://mediakix.com/2016/01/snapchat-statistics-2016-marketers-need-to-know…

Noyes, Dan. (January 4, 2018). *The Top 20 Valuable Facebook Statistics – Updated January 2018*. Retrieved from https://zephoria.com/top-15-valuable-facebook-statistics/

Newberry, Christina. (January 17, 2018). *28 Twitter Statistics All Marketers Need to Know in 2018*. Retrieved from https://blog.hootsuite.com/twitter-statistics/

Perez, Sarah. (January 23, 2015). *Pinterest Goes After the Male Demographic with Debut of New Search Filters*. Retrieved from https://techcrunch.com/2015/01/23/pinterest-goes-after-the-male-demographic-with-debut-of-new-search-filters/

Pew Research Center. (January 12, 2017). *Social Media Fact Sheet*. Retrieved from http://www.pewinternet.org/fact-sheet/social-media/

Shearer, Elisa and Gottfriend, Jeffrey. (September 7, 2017). *News Use Across Social Media Platforms 2017*. Retrieved from http://www.journalism.org/2017/09/07/news-use-across-social-media-platforms-2017/

Smith, Craig. (January 2, 2018). 220 *Amazing LinkedIn Statistics and Facts* (January 2018). Retrieved from https://expandedramblings.com/index.php/by-the-numbers-a-few-important-linkedin-stats/7/

Smith, Kit. (December 12, 2017). 39 *Fascinating and Incredible YouTube Statistics*. Retrieved from https://www.brandwatch.com/blog/36-youtube-stats-2016/

Smith, Kit. (December 17, 2017). *44 Incredible and Interesting Twitter Statistics*. Retrieved from https://www.brandwatch.com/blog/44-twitter-stats-2016/

Statistic Brain. (September 4, 2017). *Google Plus Demographics & Statistics*. Retrieved from https://www.statisticbrain.com/google-plus-demographics-statistics/

Wade, Jessica. (November 8, 2017). *Instagram Statistics 2017*. Retrieved from https://www.smartinsights.com/social-media-marketing/instagram-marketing/instagram-statistics/

Chapter 9: Analyzing the Team

Fundbox. (March 16, 2017). *Fundbox Study Reveals Crippling Effects of Late or Unpaid Invoices.* Retrieved from https://www.prnewswire. com/news-releases/fundbox-study-reveals-crippling-effects-of-late-or-unpaid-invoices-300424576.html

Chapter 10: Finding the Funding

The CMO Survey. (August, 2017). *Latest Results: August 2017.* Retrieved from https://cmosurvey.org/results/august-2017/

Deloitte. (n.d.) *The CMO Survey Results.* Retrieved on February 1, 2018, from https://cmo.deloitte.com/xc/en/pages/solutions/cmosurvey.html

Moorman, Christine and Finch, T. Austin. (January 24, 2017). *Marketing Budgets Vary by Industry.* Retrieved from http://deloitte.wsj. com/cmo/2017/01/24/who-has-the-biggest-marketing-budgets/

Moorman, Christine. (February 28, 2017). *The CMO Survey Highlights and Insights February 2017.* Retrieved from https://www.slideshare. net/christinemoorman/the-cmo-survey-highlights-and-insights-february-2017

Sorofman, Jake and McLellan, Laura. (February 13, 2017). *CMO Spend Survey 2015: Eye on the Buyer.* Retrieved from https://www.gartner.com/doc/2984821/cmo-spend-survey--eye

About the Author

Jennifer S. LeBlanc, founder and president of ThinkResults Marketing, works with CEOs and CMOs to drive results. Her client work focuses on building go-to-market and launch strategies for high-growth companies of all sizes including Microsoft Ventures/Accelerator, SAP, Intel's New Devices Group, and dozens of startups. Her proprietary methodologies have driven well over $1.5B in new funding and revenue to clients, and 10 to 100x returns for the startups she's worked with over the years.

Jennifer has received the Silicon Valley Women of Influence Award, and ThinkResults was ranked as 2017's 10th Fastest Growing Private Company in Silicon Valley by the *Silicon Valley Business Journal*. She was an advisor to President Obama, Congress and the SBA via the National Women's Business Council.

A high-energy speaker who inspires and galvanizes her audiences into action, Jennifer is the author of two books, *Launching for Revenue: How to Launch Your Product, Service or Company for Maximum Growth* and *Changing Tides: Powerful Strategies for Female Founders*.

To connect with the author for speaking, workshops, coaching and consulting questions, please visit jennifersleblanc.com.

Made in the USA
Columbia, SC
18 July 2019